The
Testimony
of
God

The Testimony of God

WATCHMAN NEE

Translated from the Chinese

Christian Fellowship Publishers, Inc.
New York

Available from the Publishers at:

11515 Allecingie Parkway
Richmond, Virginia 23235

PRINTED IN U.S.A.

TRANSLATOR'S PREFACE

We frequently mention the testimony of God, but what exactly is His testimony and what does this testimony mean to us? The testimony is the self-revelation of God. In other words, it represents God's heart desire, which is also God's requirement—or we may say, God's standard. His standard reveals himself, showing us what a God He is. When this testimony comes to man, it becomes law. On God's side, it is testimony, but on the human side, it is law.

The Lord Jesus comes to bear witness to the Father; the Holy Spirit comes to bear witness to Christ; the church is to maintain the testimony of Jesus Christ in the power of the Holy Spirit. The witnessing of Christ is none other than telling people who Christ is and what Christ is. It behooves us not to sin against this testimony—for whenever we do sin against it, our action will not easily be overlooked by God.

In this volume Watchman Nee presents in the first part the testimony of God as to what it is, how it comes to us, and what our responsibility is towards it. In the second part, he exhorts us to be faithful to the testimony which is committed to us and to finish our course triumphantly. May such faithfulness to the very end be the case in the lives of all who read the pages of this book.

CONTENTS

*1 Corinthians 2.1
**1 Timothy 1.12

This small volume is a collection of messages given in Chinese by the author on various occasions throughout his years of ministry. Because of the unity of their content, these messages are now being translated and published in single book form.

Scripture quotations are from the American Standard Version of the Bible (1901), unless otherwise indicated.

PART ONE

"THE TESTIMONY OF GOD"

1 | The Testimony of God

I am thy servant; give me understanding, that I may know thy testimonies. (Ps. 119.125)

We frequently mention the testimony of God, but what is His testimony and to what does it point?

The word "testimony" or "testimonies" is used more often in the Old Testament than in the New. Here we would take note especially of two places in the Old Testament. One is found in the Pentateuch of Moses, particularly in the Book of Exodus, where the word "testimony" is used profusely: such as in the phrases "the ark of the testimony" and "the two tables of the testimony" (see Ex. 25.22, 31.18). The other is found in Psalm 119 where the word "testimonies" is repeatedly employed. By looking closely at these two places we may have our eyes opened to know what is the real meaning of the testimony of God.

Psalm 119 refers many times to the word of God, to the precepts of God, the law of God, the statutes of God, the commandments of God, and also to the testimonies of God. The psalmist lists testimonies together with God's word, precepts, statutes, commandments, and so forth. We are exhorted to keep His testimonies in the same way as we are required to keep His word, precepts, law, statutes and commandments. It may sound a little strange to our ears when we say we must keep God's testimonies. But we find in the Bible that His testimonies are of the same nature as are His word, precepts, law, statutes and commandments.

In Exodus, Leviticus and Numbers we find not only that God's testimony stands on the same footing as His word and His law, but that even the two tables of stone on which His law was inscribed are called the two tables of the testimony and also that the ark in which the two tables were placed is called the ark of the testimony. All these things are of God's own doing.

Thus we are shown what the testimony is. The testimony is the law. In other words, it represents God's heart desire, which is also God's requirement—or may we say it, God's standard. As a matter of fact, the two tables of the testimony mentioned in Exodus picture for us a beautiful theme: the very standard of God. What is God's standard? His standard reveals himself, showing us what a God He is. And the testimony is given to us in order that we may know what is the absolute standard of God.

When this testimony comes to man, it becomes

law. On God's side, it is testimony; but on the human side, it is law. Hence law and testimony are one and the same thing though viewed differently. It is testimony with respect to God; but it becomes law with respect to man. It testifies to what God requires; it delineates what needs to be kept by man. With regard to God, testimony is His demand; with regard to man, testimony is his duty. It bears witness to the kind of God we have as over against the sort of life we humans live. When it is placed in our hand, such a testimony convicts us of our unrighteousness since we have fallen short of the divine standard. But while it remains in the Lord's hand, it reveals what a God He is. Testimony, therefore, is the self-revelation of God.

This becomes even clearer in the New Testament period. The Lord Jesus comes to bear witness to the Father; the Holy Spirit comes to bear witness to Christ; and the church is to maintain the testimony of Christ Jesus in the power of the Holy Spirit. The witnessing of Christ is none other than telling people who Christ is and what Christ is. And this is called testimony. With respect to God, this testimony is nothing less than himself; with respect to us, this testimony is a most serious thing for it becomes law to us. It behooves us not to sin against this testimony. For whenever we do sin against it, our action will not be easily overlooked by God.

Testifying for God Requires Knowing Him

We must acknowledge that this testimony is a tremendous thing. (Please note that the "testimony" referred to here is different from what is commonly known as "giving testimony.") For the primary idea surrounding this testimony is God's speaking concerning himself. By this testimony He himself tells us what a living God He is. He comes to man to bear witness to himself as to what kind of person He is. We must confess that this testimony is a spiritual reality, that which is ultimately real. Whoever fails to touch the ultimate reality does not touch the testimony. Strictly speaking, no one can bear witness for God, since from eternity to eternity the divine testimony is given by God himself. He alone can tell us what He is.

We may say many words about God and declare what a God He is, and in so doing we profess that we are testifying for Him; but all our words are of no avail. We may multiply our words ten or even a hundred times; even so, the testimony of which we have been speaking cannot be given by man: it has to come from God himself. If He himself does not speak, there will be no testimony. Do we see the gravity of this matter? If God chooses not to speak about himself, who can testify for Him? We may talk and talk, but this is useless for *we* are speaking. If God does not speak, all is vanity. As an illustration, suppose we go to a court to testify for some person. What value are our words if in spite of our eloquence the party directly involved keeps his silence and shows no expression whatsoever? Let us therefore be reminded once again that the testimony of God is God speaking of himself, and if He fails to speak, there is *no* testimony.

Hence to testify for God requires of man that he

touch God himself so as to be able to speak the words
which God wishes him to say. Man can speak only
after God is known, seen and revealed to him. Only
when he has touched this ultimate reality is he able to
open his mouth and testify for God. In case he has
not touched this reality, he will have no words to say
and therefore no testimony to give. One may spread
the commandment or statute or ordinance or word of
God, but testimony is quite a different matter. What
comes to man is commandment, statute, ordinance or
word, but testimony remains with God. All these
other matters are external whereas testimony is the
absolute reality. It consequently needs Christ, who
comes from God to bear witness for God. Then too,
it is the Holy Spirit who proceeds from Christ and
bears witness for Christ. And hence the one who
knows Christ and knows the Holy Spirit can bear
witness for God and His Christ.

Such a witness does not rely upon the man's word
or doctrine or teaching, because it is Christ himself
who has come forth. A testimony may become a doctrine, but a doctrine can never become a testimony.
When testimony is given, commandment may come
upon man for him to obey; yet this commandment is
not the testimony. This testimony is something totally
different from the testimony we commonly know of.
How often we say we cannot testify for we do not
have the experience. Yet let us realize that even experience is too small to match up with *this* testimony.
For this testimony is more than a matter of experience. It is touching the Lord himself. Yes, manward,
testimony is indeed experience; nonetheless, the term

experience is far too inadequate when discussing testimony. Because testimony is a matter of touching the
Lord, He alone can testify for himself. Since there is
none greater than God, He is the only One who can
bear witness for himself.

One of the great problems confronting the church
is the fact of too much doctrine coming from man.
People speak on many doctrines and give many teachings on the Scriptures. They tell us what we ought to
do, and what is scriptural or what is not scriptural.
They are completely immersed in matters such as
these. But true testimony is a matter of touching the
ultimate reality; only touching God himself gives the
testimony. Read again the five books of Moses and
Psalm 119, and you will discover that the way God
uses the term "testimony" is entirely different from
the way we ordinarily employ the term. Testimony is
of such immensity that it is not easily comprehended
by our mind, because it is God himself speaking, and
by which He reveals himself and also His demand.
Whoever touches this divine testimony has in reality
touched God himself.

Sinning against God Is Sinning against
the Testimony

What is meant by sinning against the testimony? It
simply means sinning against God. Whatever touches
the character or the way of God touches His testimony. God *will* have His absolute character manifested. And that which misrepresents His character
sins against His testimony. Whenever God's testi-

mony is involved, He will not overlook the event. Whatever defames or falsely represents Him, He will immediately deal with it, since it affects His character, His position, even His very self.

The Israelites Not Permitted to Enter Canaan

Several incidents in the Old Testament resulted in some very serious consequences. In Numbers 13 and 14 we find that the Lord would not let the Israelites enter Canaan. Before the people arrived at Kadesh-barnea they were always forgiven in spite of their many sins and their tempting of God in numerous ways. But when the incident at Kadesh-barnea occurred, the Lord refused to let them enter the land, and His verdict was final. Why? Because before they had reached Kadesh-barnea, they were already shown many miracles; and even at Kadesh they had become convinced that the land of Canaan was undoubtedly flowing with milk and honey; nonetheless they now considered the inhabitants of the land too strong, the cities too well-fortified, and they looked upon themselves as grasshoppers by comparison with the giant of Anak there. They were afraid and were not willing to go in. They wept and refused to move forward. Yet such weeping and fear now brought disgrace to God and affected adversely His name.

In the former days, their murmurings for food and drink did not seem to be very serious concerns to the Lord. These sins were due to human weaknesses, and God could afford to deal kindly with them: "They tempted God in their heart by asking food ac-

cording to their desire. Yea, they spake against God;
they said, Can God prepare a table in the
wilderness?'' (Ps. 78.18–19)* Did such actions by the
Israelites affect the character of the Lord? No, He
knew how their lust was aroused, and therefore He let
them travel on, but of course after He had punished
them. Not so, however, following their arrival at
Kadesh-barnea. Here it was no longer a question of
human weakness—rather, they were questioning the
power of God. The fear, the weeping, and the refusal
to enter in which they now exhibited reflected
adversely on God's character as though He—because
of His own apparent weakness—had brought them to
the place of death. At this juncture the Lord could
not forbear any longer. According to His government
He would no more bear with them. All who had
reached Kadesh-barnea and thereafter refused to go
in were forever barred from entry. Was it not most
strange that there was no possibility of repentance?
For even after they subsequently said that they would
go up, God would not change His mind. And why?
Because there is no repentance in the Lord's *government*. Whatever is decided is final. Since they had
sinned against the character of God—it being a direct
affront to Him—they were not allowed to enter the
land. This was an instance of sinning against the testimony of God.

---

*It should be noted by the reader that the phrase "Can God
. . . " should not be taken to mean here that the Israelites were
doubting the power of God but that they were challenging Him
to take action to gratify their lust.—*Translator*

The Destruction of Korah and His Company

In Numbers 16 and 17 we read of the destruction of Korah and all his company. They attacked Moses and Aaron by accusing the latter of taking too much upon themselves and lifting themselves up above the assembly of the Lord. God judged Korah and his company, and the ground opened its mouth and swallowed them up. On the next day, when the congregation of the children of Israel murmured against Moses and Aaron by saying that the latter had killed the Lord's people, there came down wrath from God upon the people. Then God spoke to Moses, instructing him that twelve rods—one for each of the twelve princes of Israel—were to be laid in the tent of meeting before the Testimony. And the man whose rod budded was thereby known to be the one chosen by God. So that in this severe judgment we can discover a great principle. If people are merely striving to be the greater among *themselves*, God will pass them over. The two brothers James and John, for example, wished to be great, yet the earth was not opened to swallow *them* up. Even during the Lord's last supper with His disciples, they were still arguing about who was the greater, but neither on that occasion did the ground open its mouth to engulf them. Why, then, must there be such severe consequence in the above incident from Numbers? There can be only one reason, which is, that they had sinned against the testimony of the Lord. For the testimony here is: that a dead person cannot serve God, only the resurrected

one can. Only in the power of resurrection can man
serve the Lord.

Apart from resurrection there is no life. At the
time of the Garden of Eden man could see the tree of
life, but today life is only found in resurrection since
death has already come in. Life today is represented
by resurrection. And hence, without resurrection no
one may approach God. The life in us which we believers know today has passed through death, therefore it is called resurrection life. How exquisite is the
word of Revelation: "I was dead, and behold, I am
alive for evermore" (1.18). Today's problem is no
longer how to keep alive but how to be raised from
among the dead. And just as our Lord is now standing on resurrection ground, so we too must stand on
the same ground. Nothing but what stands on resurrection ground may come before God. Everything
must go through death and be made alive again. How
much of our human eloquence, thought, ability,
strength and cleverness has not passed through death
and is not on resurrection ground! With the result
that these things gain for us no access to God.

Thus in the above incident concerning Aaron's
rod we are clearly shown that only what was resurrected could serve God. The rod which budded
proved beyond doubt that the resurrected one alone
was given the ministry, for without resurrection there
could be no service. Now this is testimony. This incident attests to a most important principle: that no one
can approach the Lord except on resurrection
ground. When man was first created, he was able to
draw near to God; but after his fall he could only

come by resurrection, because a sinner who would thereafter dare to approach God must die.

Resurrection is therefore the one and only condition for the service of God today. Naturally this resurrection means more than simply receiving the resurrection life; it also speaks of the working of the cross in men's lives. Just as the cross was a subtraction to the Lord Jesus, so it needs to be a subtraction to His followers as well. When the mob was intent on having the Lord crucified, they shouted: "Away with him, away with him!" So that the cross is a great subtraction, in that the old creation must all be taken away. How can the testimony of God be maintained if the rod fails to bud and the old creation does not fade away? And hence we may say that God opens just one door by which we may enter in. All who do not come in through that door must die.

The reason therefore why Korah and all his company suffered such severe judgment on that day was because they had sinned against the testimony of the Lord. God may allow certain things to pass unnoticed, but He will never let anything slip by which sins against His testimony—against His character and person. Let it be known that the basic aim of God's discipline upon us is to preserve His testimony. In other words, He does not want himself misunderstood. Concerning many people who sin, the most critical thing one can say is how bad they are, but one cannot criticize God. There are certain matters and actions which can bring adverse reflection on God; and these will not be overlooked by Him since they sin against testimony—even against God himself.

Moses Barred from Entering Canaan

From a reading of Numbers 20 we learn how Moses struck the rock with his rod twice. As a consequence, he was not allowed to enter Canaan. Even though afterwards he pleaded with God, saying "Let me go over, I pray thee" (see Deut. 3.23–27), he was still not granted permission. The forbiddance was final. Of course we understand that Moses was wrong in striking the rock with wrath instead of *speaking* to the rock as God had instructed him to do, but we still may not perceive how great a sin he had committed. Moses was a man of meekness, yet at that time he lost his temper. We have seen many meek persons losing their temper without their being seriously judged by the Lord. Why, then, was the Lord so severe with Moses who merely lost his temper once? Let us read from the Bible what God himself said: "And Jehovah said unto Moses and Aaron, Because ye believed not in me, to sanctify me in the eyes of the children of Israel, therefore ye shall not bring this assembly into the land which I have given them" (Num. 20.12). What is meant by the words "to sanctify me" not? It means "you have complicated Me"—since to sanctify God denotes to set Him apart, that is to say, to display the characteristics of God. Had Moses lost his temper ten times, people could only say that he possessed a quick temper; but his loss of control over his temper this one time affected God himself. It is as though the Lord were saying, "In your action you have drawn Me into it; you have not sanctified Me and honored Me with My rightful place."

The problem with this incident is, that while Moses was losing his temper God *at the very same time* was working—for the water came forth abundantly immediately after the rock was smitten; and so the people would obviously be confused about the situation. Moses had definitely dragged God into this awful mess, with the result that the Israelites might have thought that the Lord was a God who, like Moses, lost control of His temper. God was therefore complicated by Moses. Had Moses' wrath merely given the impression of his being a man who constitutionally had a bad temper, it would not have been so serious as to receive such a severe dealing from the Lord. But the fact that he was performing a miracle which involved the power of God being displayed at the very moment the rock was angrily struck by him might easily induce the people to conclude that the God who gave them water to drink was also a God who at that same moment chided them with wrath. Moses had so involved the Lord in his own wrath that he failed to sanctify God before the people. This is sinning against God's character, God's testimony. And the consequence of it was far too serious to be overlooked; and hence Moses was not allowed to enter Canaan.

Uzzah Smitten to Death

We can never forget the hand of Uzzah, either, in connection with this matter of sinning against the testimony. Recall how when Uzzah put forth his hand to take hold of the ark he was instantly smitten to death alongside the cart (see 2 Sam. 6.1–7). God truly vindicated himself on this occasion. We often explain that Uzzah was struck down because he stretched forth the hand of flesh to take hold of the ark. Although this is true, such an explanation and such a lesson derived therefrom is still not strong and deep enough. We must remember that the ark was the ark of the testimony. Before David was made king, the ark had been captured by the Philistines. At that time there had been no Uzzah to safeguard it; nevertheless, it was well able to defend itself. For recall that whenever in Philistia it was removed from place to place, it never once faltered, although it did not have the care of either Uzzah or any other Israelite: the Philistines could not do anything to it. Now, though, the ark was back among God's own people. Did it therefore need any man to hold it? Here must we see the sin of Uzzah. The ark was well able to defend itself among enemies; would it now require the care of man among the Lord's own people? God, you will remember, had always wanted the ark to be borne by the Levites, but the people of Israel had now put it on an oxcart. Yet should it fall, this would have to be its own business. Any stretching of the hand of man would only destroy God's testimony. Hence God would not allow Uzzah to go untouched.

Oh do let us learn a lesson before the Lord. There are many things which we must let God work out. Those who do not know Him deeply enough often try to help Him. Were we to spend a little time considering the end of those people in the past, we would notice a great principle, which is, that we cannot afford to sin against the testimony of the Lord. Whenever anyone does a thing which sins against God's character, God's authority, God's way, God's plan or God's testimony, he will be chastened by God. For He is never careless about His testimony. He will ever and always vindicate himself as the holy, mighty and living One. Because of this, may we tremble with fear before Him and never attempt anything frivolously.

Whoever Sins against the Testimony Is Chastened

We believe God frequently chastens His people for this one thing—that He wishes to vindicate himself. He clears himself of any adverse involvement with what man has done before men and also before the devil. If man is unable to maintain God's testimony, God has to come forth to defend it. But this means that man will be chastened by Him. When we sin in matters which touch only ourselves, it seems as though the Lord is not as serious concerning them as when we sin in matters which offend Him himself. In the latter case He will rise up to chasten and to declare His innocency. Let us therefore walk very softly before God. Let us not sin in anything, especially let us not sin against His testimony. Always have a heart of fear and trembling, asking the Lord to keep us from sinning, particularly from sinning against the testimony.

We have read the stories of many people in the Old Testament—such as those of Abraham, Isaac and Jacob. They were all chosen and beloved of God. Their histories reveal countless failures and defeats, yet the Lord allowed them to pass after but a little judgment. Are we surprised? Why was it so? Because their wrong acts did not sin against God's testimony. Whenever the testimony of the Lord is offended, the consequence will be most grave and terrible. In this respect there is no difference between the Old and the New Testaments, since the real difference lies only in whether the testimony is offended or respected. To sin against God's testimony is a horrible thing because He will not easily pass it by.

"They indeed for a few days chastened us as seemed good to them; but he for our profit, that we may be made partakers of his holiness" (Heb. 12.10). God chastens us for our profit that we may become partakers of His holiness. Each time He chastens us He vindicates His own self.*

Have you ever pondered over the fact that when God chastens us to vindicate himself, Satan can no longer accuse? In chastisement God shows the enemy that He, God, has no part in the matter, thus preserving His holiness. For this reason, our first reaction under chastisement should not be asking for relief but asking for help to satisfy God. Each time we come under chastisement of this nature, we may tell brothers

---

*It must be kept in mind that the author, when giving this message, was emphasizing one particular aspect of God's chastisement—namely, that which is due to an offense against God and His character; there is of course another aspect to chastisement that has to do with child-training for the positive purpose of conforming the believer to the image of God's Son. This the reader should keep in mind as he reads the paragraph to follow.—*Translator*

and sisters that this is due to our offending God in a certain matter. Our word may sound simple, but our doing this will uphold the fact that the Lord has had no part in the matter. Some brothers and sisters only know crying under chastisement. Why cry? Because the discipline is too severe? Because there is hardship? Oh, these are not for crying. We ought to see that God's chastisement, as severe and hard as it may be, is His vindication of himself. Since His name is upon us, He can easily be complicated by us. And hence He has to extricate himself from any adverse involvement which our actions may bring about. During the time of such chastisement let us bow our heads and worship God, saying: "I will gladly accept such discipline; I will gladly stand on such ground; I will gladly let the devil, the church and the world know that you have had nothing to do with it but that it is all my fault." The more we submit ourselves under God's disciplinary hand the more He is vindicated, and therefore the quicker discipline of this kind will pass away. On the other hand, the harder we try to escape such discipline and the more we struggle against it, the less we shall be able to get through.

I believe this is part of the Lord's way, the learning of which will enable Him to be glorified in our defeats and will deliver us from many unnecessary sorrows. If we live our Christian life well, we glorify God by giving thanks for His grace. If we live it poorly, we still need to glorify Him by submitting to His vindication. May the blood cover these words, for they touch upon a most serious theme.

2 | The Testimony of the Lord Jesus before the High Priest and Pilate

Scripture Reading: Matthew 26.57–66; 27.1,2,11–18; John 18.28–40; 19.7–10,12,15.

One

On the night of His betrayal, the Lord Jesus was led away, by those who seized Him, to Caiaphas the high priest. Now the chief priests and the whole council kept trying to obtain false testimony against Him in order that they might put Him to death; but they were not able to find such, even though many false witnesses came forward. One special feature about this event is to be noticed here. In such a situation of being questioned with many words and of being falsely accused of many things, Jesus answered not one word. But when the high priest asked Him to "tell . . . whether thou art the Christ, the Son of God," He replied, "Thou hast said"—with the result that the high priest seized upon this confession of His to condemn Him. On the next morning, they brought the Lord Jesus bound in order to deliver Him over to Pilate the Roman governor. Pilate questioned Him, saying: "Art thou the king of the Jews?" And Jesus said to him, "Thou sayst." Is it not rather strange that after He had so answered, Pilate judged Him to be innocent and wished to release Him? In the case of the high priest, Jesus was condemned by His having answered, "Thou hast said it"; but with Pilate, Jesus was absolved for saying essentially the same thing— "Thou sayst." These two encounters serve as a contrast. Before Caiaphas the high priest, the Lord Jesus was judged not on the question of kingship but on that of Sonship; but before Pilate the governor He was judged on the question of kingship. The questions seem to be quite apart outwardly, yet before God they are united into one. For before God, the Jews had no king other than the Son of God himself. In His two trials, therefore, the Lord Jesus answered nothing except these two questions—as to who He was and what He did.

Two

Let us notice the testimony of the Lord here. Jesus confessed before Caiaphas the high priest that He was the Son of God and before Pilate the governor that He was king. In both cases He testified to himself. When the high priest heard what the Lord testified concerning himself—together with the word, "Henceforth ye shall see the Son of man sitting at the right hand of power and coming on the clouds of heaven"—he tore his robes and declared: "He hath spoken blasphemy: what further need have we of witnesses? behold, now ye have heard the blasphemy: what think ye?" To which the council responded that he was worthy of death.

Why did they not accept this testimony given by the Lord Jesus? What was their secret thought? They had no intention of proving whether or not He was truly the Son of God because they considered His confession of being the Son of God to be one of guilt. Their aim was not at proving a fact, it was instead one of finding an excuse for condemning. Hence immediately after the Lord Jesus acknowledged himself to be the Son of God, they judged His word as blasphemy and condemned Him. This showed they had no intention of finding out whether this Man was truly the Son of God; their sole concern was to kill Him on the ground of whatever He said which could be used against Him.

They were *the* leaders of Judaism, yet they were not concerned with God's business. What they were anxious about was the detriment to themselves that was being caused by what this Man who was called the Son of God constantly said and did. If they permitted Him to continue to live, their position would be irretrievably shaken and their "authority" shattered. For this reason, they hastened to get rid of Jesus that they might preserve their personal gain. Though they pretended to show their concern over the temple by twisting the word of the Lord Jesus to make it: "I am able to destroy the temple of God and

to rebuild it in three days'' (yet in actuality the Lord
Jesus had not so spoken; see John 2.19–21), they did
not in the least mind allowing the temple to become a
robbers' den. For when the Lord had earlier come to
cleanse it of such iniquity, they instead had sought to
destroy Him (see Mark 11.17–18). They only wished
to keep the outward appearance of the temple as a
means of profiteering; they did not want the reality of
the temple lest their sins be exposed. They retained
some religious rituals but rejected the truth, even to
the point of destroying it. They unhesitatingly and
without any further inquiry judged Jesus' confession
of being the Son of God to be a crime. They considered such a confession to be taboo. Even though it
were true, it ought not be uttered. The Lord Jesus was
condemned because of this testimony. He was sen-
tenced to death not because of what He was but
because of what He testified as to himself. According
to the opinion of the council, truth should not be at-
tested to. They tried every means to overthrow this
testimony, and finally they resorted to human power
to put the Lord Jesus to death.

Three

In the morning, they brought the Lord Jesus to
Pilate. In response to the governor's asking the Lord
''Art thou the king of the Jews?'', Jesus answered,
''Sayst thou this of thyself, or did others tell it thee
concerning me?'' And Pilate replied, ''Am I a Jew?
Thine own nation and the chief priests delivered thee

unto me: what hast thou done?'' Jesus answered, "My kingdom is not of this world: if my kingdom were of this world, then would my servants fight, that I should not be delivered to the Jews: but now is my kingdom not from hence.'' Therefore Pilate said to him, "Art thou a king then?'' To this Jesus answered, "Thou sayst that I am a king. To this end have I been born, and to this end am I come into the world, that I should bear witness unto the truth. Every one that is of the truth heareth my voice.'' Pilate said to Him, "What is truth?'' But without waiting for the answer he came out to the Jews and told them, "I find no crime in him.'' And thus was the testimony which the Lord Jesus gave before Pilate.

Many of that day thought this matter of being the king of the Jews was a political problem. But the Bible shows us that when the Lord Jesus was asked by Pilate, "Art thou the king of the Jews?'', Jesus probed into the source of this word by inquiring whether this was Pilate's own understanding or something he had heard. Such inquiry was of great importance. For the Lord Jesus testified openly without any hiding that He was a king. Yet what He testified and what He was accused of were totally different. The king is closely related to the kingdom, and consequently He declared, "My kingdom is not of this world.'' Since His kingdom was not of this world, His servants had no need to fight for Him. If it had been of this world, they would have fought. But His kingdom is of God and from above; accordingly, there is no need to fight with flesh and blood. Though He is king of the Jews and He is born to be king, His kingdom has nothing to do with world politics.

Among God's children, some only know the world as a material entity. To them, to be not of the world is to be a little more careful concerning the material things. Now we are not suggesting that we should be lax with respect to the material side. Nonetheless, the biggest issue in regard to our relationship to the world is the question of source—whether we are "of" or "not of" the world. In other words, we do not at all belong to this world.

There are many things in the lives of God's children which appear to be spiritual, but oftentimes if these things are traced to their source, they would be found to have emanated from the world. Although the terms may be scriptural, the things may have their source in the world. For example, we concede that humility is a virtue, and surely it is a mode of behavior commended in the Scriptures. Nevertheless, whether the humility delineated in the Scriptures and the humility in our lives are one and the same thing may often present a real problem. Frequently, in tracking down the source of our humility, we discover it arises out of certain considerations—for instance, out of fear lest someone may lose face or we ourselves be criticized. So that this humility of ours grows out of a worldly consideration. Outwardly it may be called a virtue, but it does not originate in the kingdom which is not of this world. It has its source in this world, it being the result of mundane considerations.

Oh do let us see that a Christian who lives by God can be gentle as well as strong because he is not governed by any worldly consideration.

God's children frequently talk about being heavenly. What is meant by being heavenly? It does not necessarily signify that we are always in touch with heavenly things. It actually means that this or that comes out of heaven, that heaven is its source. Similarly, then, what is meant by being worldly? It does not have reference to our being in constant contact with the world but it speaks instead of that which comes out of the world. Let us not imagine we could be unworldly if we had less contact with the world. Having less intercourse with the things of the earth only makes us recluses—those who escape from reality. No, such conduct will not make us not of the world. We instead need God's light, because we are originally of the world. And under His enlightenment, we will be enabled to see just how many earthly reasons do govern much of our goodness. There is a reason for each action, and frequently these reasons originate from the world. How many goodnesses of ours may give the appearance of being spiritual, but in actuality they may be merely worldly "spirituality." There is neither testimony or reality in them.

The Lord Jesus declared that His kingdom is not of this world. He reigns and rules over a realm which is not of this earth. His kingdom has nothing in common with the worldly one. And for this very reason, therefore, our problem is not concerned with whether we have left the world or not but is concerned with how much of the world may still be in us. May God be gracious to us that we may not be affected by the world at all.

Four

The Lord Jesus came to this world to bear witness to the truth. Those hypocrites of that time tried to get rid of Him because their own conduct was evil and because they loved darkness instead of light (see John 3.19). But the Lord Jesus did not yield to their evil power. He kept silent while railed at but gave an excellent testimony to the truth when His person and work were called into question. Though He traveled over an uncommon path and seemingly appeared to have accomplished nothing, He is today seated at the right hand of Power and will one day come on the clouds of heaven. Praise the Lord! All who follow Him must pay attention to His testimony.

3 | The Testimony of Jesus Christ

> Who bare witness of the word of God, and of the
> testimony of Jesus Christ, even of all things that he saw.
> (Rev. 1.2)

In the book of Revelation, "the testimony of Jesus Christ" is mentioned several times. It was because of the testimony of Jesus Christ that the apostle John was exiled to the island of Patmos (Rev. 1.9). Because of "the testimony" which they had maintained, the saints of old were slain (Rev. 6.9). Satan attacks fiercely those who "hold the testimony of Jesus" (Rev. 12.17). At the return of the Lord, they who hold fast to "the testimony of Jesus" shall reign with Him. Furthermore, an angel declared to John that "the testimony of Jesus is the spirit of prophecy" (Rev. 19.10). And finally, Paul in one of his epistles also had this to say: "even as the testimony of Christ was confirmed in you" (1 Cor. 1.6). What, then, is the testimony of Jesus Christ?

It would take some little time to answer this question fully. We therefore can only briefly explain here its essence. The testimony of Jesus Christ includes four aspects: first, who Jesus is—that is to say, what He formerly was, and what He now is; second, what His relationship to man is; third, what He has done and accomplished on the cross; and fourth, what His relationship to God's eternal purpose is. We believe that these four aspects embrace the full scope of the testimony of Jesus Christ. Much could be said about these four aspects, but we will only state them concisely.

First, who Jesus formerly was and who He is now. These matters touch on the Person of Christ, which subject occupies a most prominent place in spiritual theology. Let us not deem theology to be merely learning a special technique. We will discover that the deepest, sharpest and most subtle of the devil's devices is to attack the Person of Christ. He seeks every opportunity to lead men astray towards some profound and philosophical approaches to the Person of Christ. If he is able to entice a godly believer to fall on this point, he can destroy the life ministry of that individual. Do keep well in mind that the devil plots with all his cunning to ensnare God's children on this very issue. The farther we follow the Lord, the keener will Satan tempt us concerning the Person of Christ. For he is fully aware that if he strikes God's children on this point, he strikes at the very heart of all issues.

Were you to be seduced to doubt the Person of Christ, your whole being would be finished before

God. A slight questioning or a little error in your talk in regard to the Person of Christ will finish you in terms of being used in the hand of God. The devil focuses his attacks on consecrated believers to lure them away from the straight path of the truth concerning this matter. Because of this, we must judge carefully the so-called theological views of men, that we may not be trapped in Satan's net.

Who Jesus is—this is the foundation of the testimony. All false teachings and destructive doctrines assault directly or indirectly this central theme: they attack the Person of Christ. Many try to interpret Him in a roundabout way; at the end we will discover that they neither confess Christ as God nor allow others to acknowledge Him as God. Hence the first aspect of the testimony of Jesus Christ is concerned with His Person.

Second, what the relationship of Christ to man is. One term may be used to explain and to define His relationship to man, and that is the word "representative." Christ has done things which exceed any power of man and that are impossible to him. He is God, therefore He acts like God. However, Christ does all things for man. He joins himself to man by becoming flesh. He is the mystery of godliness (1 Tim. 3.16). He has four limbs and five sensory organs just as we have. He becomes one of us, therefore He can be our Representative. His life, His work, His death, burial, resurrection and ascension, and His present position and work in heaven are all representative in nature. And hence the testimony of Jesus Christ includes His relationship with man in whatever He represents both now and before.

Third, what the Lord Jesus has accomplished on the cross. This covers His death, burial, resurrection and reigning. All these are universal in character—that is to say, they are all-inclusive. His death is an all-inclusive one, and so are His burial, His resurrection and His reigning all-inclusive. This is the testimony of Jesus Christ.

And fourth, as to His relationship to God's eternal purpose, we can say that God has ordained in eternity that the Lord Jesus shall be the Head over all things. He is the King of kings. This too is the testimony of Jesus Christ.

We believe the four aspects which we have just mentioned comprise the testimony of Jesus Christ since they include all the contents of the Bible. You can draw a line from the Old Testament to the New Testament, from Genesis to Revelation, and link up these four cardinal matters. Today, the testimony of Jesus Christ is deposited in a vessel which is called the church, the body of Christ. And it is deposited in the following fashion: first, this testimony is the sum of all the revealed truth; and second, this testimony is the power of the truth as incorporated in the vessel. For this testimony of Jesus Christ as deposited in the vessel of the church is the same truth which the Holy Spirit has wrought out in Jesus Christ. It is therefore not a kind of objective truth for the mind to comprehend but is that truth becoming our life, our nature and our experience through the working of the Holy Spirit in us. And thus the testimony is deposited in that vessel which is the church. The Holy Spirit reveals and incorporates this testimony in the church, which is the body of Christ. And we who have believed in Jesus are members of this body.

Oh! Has the Holy Spirit revealed the Lord Jesus to you? You do not merely agree to what others have told you about the Lord Jesus as the Son of God; you believe Him to be God's Son because the Holy Spirit has revealed Him to you.

As to the Lord's representative work, do you not see this aspect of the testimony by the agency of the Holy Spirit? Are you seeing continuously what Christ represented in the past and what He represents today? And has that which you have seen become your life?

Let us understand that all these aspects of the testimony need to be perceived clearly. The Lord Jesus is our Representative at the right hand of God. There He represents us in all which God may require of us, be it moral or spiritual perfection. We are perfect and complete in Christ before God (Col. 1.28). God has already found a perfect man in the manhood of Jesus Christ. He has reckoned the Lord's perfection to be ours, He has put the Lord's perfection into our accounts. He has no more need to find a perfect man, because He has already obtained that Man. It is now the work of the Holy Spirit to impart that Man's perfection to us. Through our faith and obedience the Holy Spirit is able to impart Christ to us. And thus Christ becomes a part of us. This requires the work of the Holy Spirit's revelation and incorporation. Not an ideal, nor a theory, neither a creed. We will perceive the difference if we have really seen. We therefore insist on the need for the Holy Spirit's revelation and incorporation.

Concerning what the Lord Jesus has done on the cross, it too needs the revelation of the Holy Spirit to make it our portion. We must see that the Lord Jesus not only died *for* us but also died *as* us. Has the Spirit of God given you such revelation that you know that when Christ died you too died, that when He was buried you too were buried, that when He was resurrected you reappeared in Him? On resurrection ground the judgment is over, and there is no more condemnation. These may possibly be only in the Bible for us, but let us see that they may also be revealed in us, thus becoming a part of our real life.

The testimony of Jesus Christ is deposited in a vessel; the church which is the body of Christ is that vessel. We are members of Christ's body. We are called in order for the truth of the testimony in the vessel to be revealed and incorporated in us. For this reason we must

contend earnestly for the faith which was once for all delivered unto the saints. For there are certain men crept in privily, even they who were of old written beforehand unto this condemnation, ungodly men, turning the grace of our God into lasciviousness, and denying our only Master and Lord, Jesus Christ. (Jude 3–4)

4 | The Ark: the Center of the Tabernacle

Scripture Reading: Exodus 25.10–22.

The ark occupies a most significant place in the Bible. It was the first item mentioned by God when He ordered Moses to build the tabernacle. On the day the tabernacle was set up it was the only thing in the holiest of all, although in the court were found the altar of the burnt-offering and the laver while in the holy place were found the candlestick, the table with the shewbread, and the golden altar of incense (see Ex. 40.17–33). There in the holiest place God met with men, and from the mercy-seat of the ark between the two cherubim He spoke to them. The ark was therefore the center of the tabernacle.

One

Let us first look at its name. In the book of Exo-

dus its name is "ark" or "ark of the testimony." It
had yet to take on the name of the "ark of the covenant." Its very name and its location in the tabernacle
shows that God's testimony is in the midst of the people of Israel. Where the ark is, there is God's presence. Where it is, there also is the law of God. In the
book of Numbers the ark is given another name—the
ark of the covenant (see 10.33, 14.44). This indicates
the relationship between the ark and the covenant.
Wherever the ark is, there is the covenant of the
Lord. Further on, in the book of Samuel, it receives
still another new designation. It is called the "ark of
God" (see 1 Sam. 4.11,13,17,19,21,22). This symbol-
izes the fact that where the ark is, there also is the
presence of God. The ark represents God. Its presence with the people attests to the presence of God
with them.

Two

Let us further inquire as to what the ark typifies.
Quite simply, it typifies the Lord Jesus: (1) The ark in
the tabernacle signified the presence of God with His
people. Similarly, the Lord Jesus comes forth to mark
God's presence with us today, and hence He is called
Immanuel (Matt. 1.23). Wherever He is, there also is
God. (2) The ark of the Old Testament was in the holiest of all; and Christ is today in the heavenly sanctuary (Heb. 8.2, cf. 9.24). (3) When God commanded
the Israelites to build the tabernacle, the first thing He
mentioned was the ark. And this intimates that the
Lord Jesus is the center of all things. (4) The ark was

made of acacia wood, overlaid with pure gold within and without. Acacia wood is very sturdy, so it can suggest the humanity of our Lord. And pure gold in the Scriptures always stands for God's righteousness, God's glory and everything pertaining to God; it thus indicates the divinity of our Lord. Christ is both man and God; He has human nature as well as divine nature.

Much else about the ark also speaks of Christ, as can be seen in the following paragraphs.

The ark was two cubits and a half long, a cubit and a half wide, and a cubit and a half high. Upon it was located the mercy-seat which served as a cover to the ark. It was made of pure gold and was of the same length and width as the ark. In addition, two cherubim of gold of beaten work were set at the two ends of the mercy-seat, with their wings spread out on high and covering the mercy-seat. These two cherubim faced the mercy-seat as well as each other (and we know that the cherubim manifested the glory of God —see Ez. 9.3, Heb. 9.5). God had said to Moses, "There I will meet with thee, and I will commune with thee from above the mercy-seat, from between the two cherubim which are upon the ark of the testimony, of all things which I will give thee in commandment unto the children of Israel" (Ex. 25.22). From there He would guide them henceforth. During the Old Testament period all the grace of God flowed from the ark; and likewise, during the New Covenant period, it is all given to us through Christ. We are told in Leviticus 16 that once a year in the seventh month on the great day of atonement the high priest would take the blood of the bullock and of the goat into the holiest of all and sprinkle it upon the mercy-seat. In like manner the Lord has accomplished the work of redemption by the shedding of His blood, and His blood speaks continually to God for our forgiveness since the work of redemption is already done. To put it simply, the ark typified how grace is given to us through Christ. Having Christ we have the presence of God with us: because of Him we may receive God's guidance.

At the four feet of the ark were four rings of gold, and the staves of acacia wood overlaid with gold were put into these rings to bear the ark. The staves remained in the rings of the ark: they were not to be taken from it. This meant that the ark might be carried out at any time. Hence the ark had a double use: On the one hand, it was the center of worship, having been placed in the holiest of all where God and men met. If anyone desired to worship God he had to go before the ark to worship, for without it no worship was possible. On the other hand, it served as the guide to God's people—it went ahead, with the people of Israel following suit (see Num. 10.33, Joshua 3.3). They could not go just anywhere they wished; they were required to follow the lead of the ark. Here we see symbolically how Christ leads us in the way that lies before us.

How did the ark travel? Here is what the Scriptures say:

When the camp setteth forward, Aaron shall go

in, and his sons, and they shall take down the veil
of the screen, and cover the ark of the testimony
with it, and shall put thereon a covering of sealskin, and shall spread over it a cloth all of blue,
and shall put in the staves thereof. (Num. 4.5–6)

We are plainly told here that wherever the ark was
to travel, there would be three layers of covering over
it: first, the veil which separated the holiest of all
from the holy place was taken down and used to
cover the ark; second, a covering of sealskin was put
on; and third, a cloth all of blue was spread over it.
As the ark was taken out, it became as it were the time
to proclaim Christ: for we learn from the New Testament that the veil pointed to Christ's flesh (see Heb.
10.20). And now that it is already rent (see Mark
15.38), the Christ whom we today proclaim is thus
One who is most approachable. Sealskin presents a
rugged appearance, thereby expressing in type the
holiness of our Lord—how He was rejected of men.
The cloth all of blue finds its spiritual significance in
the fact of its color. Blue in the Bible represents that
which is heavenly (for the sky is blue) just as white
stands for righteousness, golden stands for the glory
of God, and purple signifies authority. The Christ
whom we follow seems to be lacking in outward
beauty just as does sealskin, yet He is heavenly as pic-
tured for us by the cloth all of blue. Though He is rejected of men, He nonetheless is well-pleasing to
God. To sum up, then, the Christ whom we proclaim
is the Lord who is approachable, rejected of men, but
well-pleasing to God.

Three

Now let us look into a little of the history of the ark, by means of which we may perceive not only the relationship between the ark and the people of Israel but also that between Christ and us.

The Ark Crossing the River Jordan

How did the people of Israel cross the Jordan River when they entered Canaan?

> And Joshua said, Hereby ye shall know that the living God is among you. . . . Behold, the ark of the covenant of the Lord of all the earth passeth over before you into the Jordan. . . . And it shall come to pass when the soles of the feet of the priests that bear the ark of Jehovah, the Lord of all the earth, shall rest in the waters of the Jordan, that the waters of the Jordan shall be cut off, even the waters that come down from above; and they shall stand in one heap. . . . When the people removed from their tents, to pass over the Jordan, the priests that bare the ark of the covenant being before the people; and when they that bare the ark were come unto the Jordan, and the feet of the priests that bare the ark were dipped in the brink of the water (for the Jordan overfloweth all its banks all the time of harvest), that the waters which came down from above stood, and rose up in one heap, a great way off, at Adam, the city that is beside Zarethan; and those that went down toward the sea of the Arabah, even the Salt Sea, were wholly cut off: and the people passed over right against Jericho. And the priests that bare the

ark of the covenant of Jehovah stood firm on dry
ground in the midst of the Jordan; and all Israel
passed over on dry ground, until all the nation
were passed clean over the Jordan. (Joshua
3.10–17)

This passage in the Bible tells us how the ark led
the people of Israel into Canaan. The ark was the last
out of water as well as the first into the water. From
this we realize that a power stronger than death led
the Israelites safely over the river Jordan. In like manner, we who have died have also been raised up with
Christ, just as Israel passed through the "death" of
Jordan under the leadership of the ark.

The Ark in the Tent at Shiloh

After the children of Israel entered Canaan and
the war was over, the whole congregation assembled
at Shiloh to set up the tent of meeting there (see
Joshua 18.1). When Eli the priest was old, his two
sons had become base men. They did not know Jehovah, yet they served as priests. Eli could do nothing
about it, for he honored his sons above God. And
hence a man of God afterwards prophesied this:
"And thou shalt behold the affliction of my habita-
tion" (1 Sam. 2.32). This meant that God would depart from the tent.

And the word of Jehovah was precious in those
days; there was no frequent vision. And it came to
pass at that time, when Eli was laid down in his

place (now his eyes had begun to wax dim, so that he could not see), and the lamp of God was not yet gone out, and Samuel was laid down to sleep, in the temple of Jehovah, where the ark of God was; that Jehovah called Samuel. (1 Sam. 3.1–4)

Though the lamp had not yet gone out before the ark in God's sanctuary, and the outward form of the tent continued as before, the presence of God would nonetheless soon depart. Then too, at that moment, God did not call Eli but instead called Samuel; He did not give His word to Eli but gave it to Samuel instead. Thereafter He laid Eli aside and chose the child Samuel. He established the latter as a prophet in Israel (1 Sam. 3.20).

Not long afterwards the ark was to depart from the tent at Shiloh. It is recorded in 1 Samuel 4 that "when the people were come into the camp, the elders of Israel said, Wherefore hath Jehovah smitten us to-day before the Philistines? Let us fetch the ark of the covenant of Jehovah out of Shiloh unto us, that it may come among us, and save us out of the hand of our enemies" (v.3). As the people of Israel were engaged in battle with the Philistines, they thought that if only they brought in the ark they could be victorious. And so they removed the ark from the tent of God in Shiloh to their battle camp. When the ark came into the camp, all Israel shouted with a great shout (1 Sam. 4.5). We thus see that in time of trouble the people thought of taking advantage of the ark; but as a consequence, even the ark was taken captive. They supposed that with the ark among them God was bound to help them, for how could He ever forsake it? Yet God did not do what they had expected. He let them be defeated and even allowed the ark to be captured by the enemies (see 1 Sam. 4.10–11).

Oh how very serious is this matter. If anyone should imagine that he will be victorious by vainly repeating such words as "I have God"—"In the name of the Lord"—"God surely is with us"—he commits the same error as the Israelites of old. The nation of Israel was beaten before the Philistines because they forgot to deal with their sins. They did not keep in mind that as long as their sins were left undealt with they would never be victorious. They ignored the fact of their rebellion against God while they dreamed of victory by holding on to the ark. How tragically they were mistaken! Nobody can use the ark in this way.

Let us always remember that spiritual things are not subject to the use of the flesh, neither is the name of Christ ever to be used by the flesh. Should any contemplate taking advantage of spiritual things or making use of the Lord's name, he will be totally defeated. Not knowing that the glory of the Lord had already departed, the people of Israel thought of using God's ark. God, however, permitted His ark to be taken captive. Let us understand that the Lord did not forsake the tent of Shiloh because the ark had been taken captive; rather, the ark was captured because the Lord had first abandoned the tent at Shiloh (cf. Ps. 78.60–61). Once God's ark left the tent of Shiloh, it never again returned to it.

The Ark among the Philistines

What happened to the ark after it was carried away to the land of the Philistines? Let us once again be reminded by this event what we earlier learned, that the ark was well able to protect itself.

> Now the Philistines had taken the ark of God, and they brought it from Ebenezer unto Ashdod. And the Philistines took the ark of God, and brought it into the house of Dagon, and set it by Dagon. And when they of Ashdod arose early on the morrow, behold, Dagon was fallen upon his face to the ground before the ark of Jehovah. And they took Dagon, and set him in his place again. And when they arose early on the morrow morning, behold, Dagon was fallen upon his face to the ground before the ark of Jehovah; and the head of Dagon and both the palms of his hands lay cut off upon the threshold; only the stump of Dagon was left to him. . . . But the hand of Jehovah was heavy upon them of Ashdod, and he destroyed them, and smote them with tumors, even Ashdod and the borders thereof. (1 Sam. 5.1-6)

The men of Ashdod were terrified and so they sent and gathered all the lords of the Philistines to themselves to counsel them as to what they should do. The decision was to remove the ark of God to Gath. And so it was that after the ark arrived there, the men of the city both small and great were struck down with tumors. They therefore sent the ark of God to Ekron, but the Ekronites cried out: "They have brought about the ark of the God of Israel to us, to slay us and our people" (v.10). They too sent and gathered together all the lords of the Philistines, asking to have the ark sent back to its original place. Meanwhile the ark of Jehovah had been in the country of the Philistines seven months.

How did they finally send back the ark of the God of Israel? The priests and the diviners among them invented a new and singular way: (1) Build a new cart, put the ark of Jehovah in it, and have it drawn by two milch cows which would have their calves sent home from them. (2) Prepare also a trespass-offering in the form of five golden tumors and five golden mice and place them in a coffer by the side of the ark which would be on the cart. They then suggested to the Philistines to watch, and "if it goeth up by the way of its own border to Beth-shemesh, then he [Jehovah] hath done us this great evil: but if not, then we shall know that it is not his hand that smote us; it was a chance that happened to us" (6.9). Now we know that a miracle happened, for the cart drawn by these two milch cows went straight along the highway till it stopped in the border of Beth-shemesh. By this the lords of the Philistines were fully convinced. And it is for this reason that we said earlier that the ark of God was well able to protect itself.

The Ark in Beth-shemesh

What occurred after the ark arrived in Beth-shemesh? "And they of Beth-shemesh were reaping their wheat harvest in the valley; and they lifted up their eyes, and saw the ark, and rejoiced to see it" (1 Sam. 6.13). But a tragedy followed, for the Lord

smote of the men of Beth-shemesh, because they
had looked into the ark of Jehovah, he smote of
the people seventy men, and fifty thousand men:
and the people mourned, because Jehovah had
smitten the people with a great slaughter. And the
men of Beth-shemesh said, Who is able to stand
before Jehovah, this holy God? and to whom shall
he go up from us? And they sent messengers to the
inhabitants of Kiriath-jearim, saying, The
Philistines have brought back the ark of Jehovah;
come ye down, and fetch it up to you. (6.19–21)

The presence of Christ is indeed most blessed;
nevertheless, people must also be holy. Because they
looked at the ark of God casually without any fear
of Him in their hearts, God killed many of the men
of Beth-shemesh. And for that reason they did not
want to have the ark among them. How very sad that
instead of dealing with the cause of chastening, the
people of Beth-shemesh refused the presence of the
Lord.

The Ark in Kiriath-jearim

What was the attitude of the men of Kiriath
jearim towards the ark?

And the men of Kiriath-jearim came, and fetched
the ark of Jehovah and brought it into the house
of Abinadab in the hill, and sanctified Eleazar his
son to keep the ark of Jehovah. And it came to
pass, from the day that the ark abode in Kiriath-
jearim, that the time was long; for it was twenty
years: and all the house of Israel lamented after
Jehovah. (1 Sam. 7.1–2)

The ark went out of Shiloh never to return again. Instead, it stayed at Kiriath-jearim in the house of Abinadab for twenty years. The tent was in Shiloh, but no ark was there. How empty Shiloh was. Now, though, the house of Abinadab was privileged with the Lord's presence. We need to underscore the fact that the ark no longer returned to Shiloh and to ask this sobering question of ourselves: Are we like the men of Beth-shemesh who were afraid of the Lord's presence, or are we like the men of Kiriath-jearim who welcomed the presence of the Lord?

The Ark in the House of Obed-edom

Twenty years later David became king. He immediately desired to have the ark removed to Jerusalem. "And David consulted with the captains of thousands and of hundreds, even with every leader. And David said . . . Let us bring again the ark of our God to us: for we sought not unto it in the days of Saul" (1 Chron. 13.1–3). It was right and good for David to think of bringing the ark of God to Jerusalem. But how did he and the people make this transfer?

> And they set the ark of God upon a new cart, and brought it out of the house of Abinadab that was in the hill: and Uzzah and Ahio, the sons of Abinadab, drove the new cart. . . . And David and all the house of Israel played before Jehovah with all manner of instruments made of fir-wood, and with harps, and with psalteries, and with timbrels, and with castanets, and with cymbals. (2 Sam. 6.3–5)

Quite unexpectedly, however, a terrible thing happened at this time of great rejoicing.

> And when they came to the threshing-floor of Nacon, Uzzah put forth his hand to the ark of God, and took hold of it; for the oxen stumbled. And the anger of Jehovah was kindled against Uzzah; and God smote him there for his error; and there he died by the ark of God. . . . And David was afraid of Jehovah that day; and he said, How shall the ark of Jehovah come unto me? So David would not remove the ark of Jehovah unto him into the city of David; but David carried it aside into the house of Obed-edom the Gittite. And the ark of Jehovah remained in the house of Obed-edom the Gittite three months: and Jehovah blessed Obed-edom, and all his house. (2 Sam. 6.6–11)

David did not inquire into the cause for the stumbling of the oxen; instead, he refused to bring the ark into the city of David simply because Uzzah was slain. But note that the house of Obed-edom welcomed the ark, with the result that his house was blessed of God abundantly. Again we need to inquire: Will we decline the presence of the Lord should we ever find ourselves being dealt with by God? Or will we, like the house of Obed-edom, welcome His presence?

Wherein lay David's fault? When he wished to bring the ark of God to Jerusalem, he failed to search through the book of the Law to find out how the ark should be carried but instead consulted with the captains of the thousands and of the hundreds. Accord-

ing to the record of Numbers 4.4–15, the ark was to
be borne by the Levites. God had never instructed
Israel to draw the ark on an ox-cart; this David and
his counselors learned from the uncircumcised Philistines. Since the Philistines knew nothing, they were
excused by God. But for David to follow the way of
the Philistines rather than the command of the Lord
was unpardonable. This ought to teach us that if we
invent a new way to express our zeal for God other
than that which is defined in the Bible and conforms
to His will, we shall not be able to maintain it for any
length of time, for before long something is bound to
happen. At first there may be music and dancing,
great enthusiasm and big crowds, but soon all will
cease. Whatever is motivated simply by temporary
passion is not pleasing to the Lord.

In all matters concerning the believer's personal
and church life, God does not permit any touch of the
flesh of man nor will He allow anyone to alter what
He has appointed. It is undeniable that Uzzah put
forth his hand in order to steady the ark (doubtless
out of his love and zeal for it). Yet we know that God
was not pleased, because He would not permit Uzzah
to touch the ark with the hand of flesh. In other
words, the Lord will not tolerate any flesh to maintain our error. You may consider your thought to be
better than God's appointed way; nevertheless, you
are prohibited from going your way. You can only
follow what God has ordained; otherwise, you will
receive the consequence of the Lord's judgment.

Some will perhaps therefore ask why we do not see
God's judgment in the church where many are substi-

tuting God's will with fleshly means? Let us answer this by saying, *with fear and trembling*, that if it is not due to the fact that the time has not yet come for God to judge the situation, then it must be for the reason that the ark (that is, God's presence) has already departed from the midst. May we never be tempted to mock the Lord because of His forbearance and patience.

The Ark in the Tent of David

Being ignorant of the cause for why God struck Uzzah to death, David dared not bring the ark to Jerusalem. But when he was told that Jehovah had blessed the house of Obed-edom because of the ark, he went down and brought up the ark from that house into the city of David with joy (see 2 Sam. 6.12 and 1 Chron. 15.25). This time, however, was different from the previous episode. For on this occasion David carefully prepared for the bringing up of the ark, saying that "none ought to carry the ark of God but the Levites: for them hath Jehovah chosen to carry the ark of God, and to minister unto him for ever" (1 Chron. 15.2). By now he had learned the lesson. Formerly he thought he could do what the Philistines had done; this time he knew that he must serve God in God's way, not in man's. So that now he had the Levites carry the ark. And the result was that

> they brought in the ark of God, and set it in the midst of the tent that David had pitched for it: and they offered burnt-offerings and peace-offerings

before God. And when David had made an end of offering the burnt-offering and the peace-offerings, he blessed the people in the name of Jehovah. (1 Chron. 16.1–2)

Solomon and the Ark

The ark had yet another episode. "And the king [Solomon] went to Gibeon to sacrifice there; for that was the great high place: a thousand burnt-offerings did Solomon offer upon that altar" (1 Kings 3.4). By night Jehovah appeared to him in a dream. He asked the Lord for wisdom, and wisdom was given to him together with other things which had not been asked for. What did Solomon then do after he awoke? "And he came to Jerusalem, and stood before the ark of the covenant of Jehovah, and offered up burnt-offerings, and offered peace-offerings, and made a feast to all his servants" (see 1 Kings 3.5–15).

At this point we need to read 2 Chronicles 1.3–4:

So Solomon, and all the assembly with him, went to the high place that was at Gibeon; for there was the tent of meeting of God, which Moses the servant of Jehovah had made in the wilderness. But the ark of God had David brought up from Kiriath-jearim to the place that David had prepared for it; for he had pitched a tent for it at Jerusalem.

At that time the tent was already in Gibeon, but the ark was not there. The problem now was: in Gibeon was the tent whereas in Jerusalem was the ark. The first thing Solomon did after he received wisdom was to return to Jerusalem and offer sacrifices before the ark. Never again did he continue to offer them in Gibeon. This marked a great turning point in Solomon's life. By all outward appearance it would seem that the tent at Shiloh had *everything*. Did it not contain the brazen altar, the laver, the candlestick, the table with the shewbread, and the golden altar of incense? (For we must understand that the tent at Gibeon was the one originally located in Shiloh, since 2 Chronicles 1 states distinctly that the tent in Gibeon was that "which Moses the servant of Jehovah had made in the wilderness"—v.3.) *But*, one thing was missing, which was the ark. People consider its absence as of no importance, not recognizing that the ark represents the presence of God. However good the rest may be, neither God's heart nor our hearts will be satisfied if His presence is missing.

Before the Lord had appeared to him, Solomon did not realize or sense the significance of the ark; but once he experienced the Lord's appearance, he became aware of the preciousness of the presence of the Lord over and above all other things. With the result that he immediately returned to Jerusalem and offered sacrifices before the ark of Jehovah. In Gibeon Solomon had only offered burnt-offerings; but now he offered burnt-offerings and peace-offerings and made a feast for all his servants. Oh, to worship before God is true worship, to commune with God is true communion, and to rejoice in God's presence is true joy. This is what Solomon had experienced, which experience is shared by many who know the

Lord. And after Solomon had built the holy temple, he placed the ark in it. And the ark became the center of the holy temple (see 2 Chron. 5.1-9). *O Ark of God, Thou Precious Ark, all who know You will seek after You and worship before You.*

Four

Having reviewed so much concerning the history of the ark, we would now like to understand more fully the relationship between Christ and the church. We have already seen that the ark typifies Christ. And the crossing of Jordan by the ark signifies the death and resurrection of our Lord. So that after knowing the Lord's death and resurrection ourselves, we can begin to proclaim Him, telling people that the veil has been rent and that Christ has opened for us a new and living way which leads directly to God. We also inform people that the Christ we proclaim is despised by men but exalted by God; He is despised like the sealskin but He is well-pleasing to God as the cloth of blue; He is the glorious Christ.

At the beginning the church announced a heavenly Christ. This, however, suffered some change even during the days of the Apostles. For at Paul's time, there were already some who preached "a different gospel" (Gal. 1.6-7). Peter, too, saw this, and warned against "destructive heresies" (2 Peter 2.1-3). Moreover, John exhorted the believers to watch for "the deceiver and the anti-christ" (2 John 7). All these admonitions give us some indication as to the

beginning of the confusing of the word of the Lord.
Constantine was raised up as the Roman Caesar and
shortly thereafter he made Christianity the state
religion. The bishop in Rome later became the titular
head of the whole Catholic system. The name of
Christ, which ought to be exclusively in the church,
fell—at that juncture—outside the pale of the church.
Such an event was not unlike what had occurred with
respect to the ark of old. The ark which was originally
in Shiloh had thence been removed to the Philistines.
And once the ark had left Shiloh, it never again returned there. Recall the words of God in the mouth of
Jeremiah: "Then will I make this house [Solomon's
temple] like Shiloh, and will make this city a curse to
all the nations of the earth" (Jer. 26.6). What was
later to happen to the temple had happened to the
tabernacle at Shiloh; namely, that though the tent
had still remained standing in Shiloh, it had been forsaken by God since His presence (the ark) was no
longer there.

Oh how the children of God need revelation, the
kind of revelation which Solomon had received. The
Lord had appeared to him and had opened his eyes to
see the preciousness of the ark and the vanity of the
tent *without* the ark. And as a consequence, what a
great change had come to his life.

Let me ask, What is it that you desire—the ark of
God or the tent without the ark? Do you choose
Christ in a religious form but without Christ himself?
We must consider whether we honor the Lord and
make Him the center or that we merely want to main-

tain the tent of Shiloh void of the ark. People always
treasure the tent in Shiloh and hold tenaciously on to
it. They assume that once it becomes the holy temple,
it forever will be. Such an assumption is not true,
however, for Jeremiah prophesied, "Trust ye not in
lying words, saying, The temple of Jehovah, the temple of Jehovah, the temple of Jehovah, are these"
(Jer. 7.4). God reproved the people of Israel because
they cared for nothing but trusting in lying words.
Three times was the phrase "the temple of Jehovah"
emphatically repeated by the prophet. Who among
Israel really knew that the temple became the temple
of Jehovah only because God was its center? If God
were to depart from the temple, that temple would be
nothing but an ordinary building.

Oh do let us recognize that what is precious is the
ark and not the tent, because the ark is the center of
the tent. Our question must come down to this, then:
Is Christ truly the center or is there merely an empty
tent? If we truly appreciate Christ, we need to look
for the place where He is actually the center. Wherever the name of Christ is, there we should be too.
Does the place where you are now take Him as the
center? If so, let us praise and thank God. But if not,
may God open our eyes that we may immediately return to "the Jerusalem that is above" (Gal. 4.26) and
worship before the ark of God's presence as did Solomon after he received the revelation. And if we do
that, we shall realize how vain was our former zealous
service; we shall come to enjoy the joy and rest before
the ark; and we shall begin to have true service and

worship. May we all have that revelation of seeing the preciousness of the Lord, of making Him the treasure and the center, of offering up the burnt-offering of consecration, and of living for Him and for His satisfaction!

5 | According to Pattern

Who serve that which is a copy and shadow of the heavenly things, even as Moses is warned of God when he is about to make the tabernacle: for, See, saith he, that thou make all things according to the pattern that was showed thee in the mount. (Heb. 8.5)

Keep back thy servant also from presumptuous sins; let them not have dominion over me: then shall I be upright, and I shall be clear from great transgression. (Ps. 19.13)

One

The most important element in spiritual work is to know "the pattern of the mount." Unquestionably there are a number of things vital to spiritual effectiveness and divine acceptance; but among them "the pattern of the mount" may be deemed the most fundamental. It is essentially the counsel of God; the lack of its understanding rules out the possibility of doing God's work.

The book of Hebrews tells us that the tabernacle was made according to the pattern God had shown Moses on Mount Sinai. Before he built the tabernacle, Moses had to remain on the mountain for forty days and nights in order to receive from God the pattern of the tabernacle. There was a definite design for everything in the tabernacle, from the holy place to the altar, for every layer of the coverings, for every kind of material used, and for every variety of colors chosen. Nothing was left to personal discretion; all was made to order. Every piece of furniture in the tabernacle—including the altar, the laver, the table, the candlestick, the censer, the ark, and so forth— was made according to the specifications laid down by God with respect to its material, measure and color. Not a single aspect was built out of Moses' own idea.

In like manner, God has His foreordained plan as to the work of the building of the church. Regardless of large or small matters, He has His own specific way. As Moses was not responsible for the design of the tabernacle but only responsible to build it according to the pattern of the mount, so the glory of a servant of Christ lies not in his ingenuity in doing God's work but rather in his careful execution of what he understands to be the will of God. To know the Lord's counsel and to execute accordingly is the glory of Christ's servant.

A sister who has served the Lord for many years

once said, "Man has absolutely no liberty in God's work." When Moses built the tabernacle, he had no freedom in deciding whether a small nail should be made of silver or of gold. He made every item according to what the Lord had commanded.

Now the man Moses was very meek (Num. 12.3). Yet what is meekness? It is tenderness, which is the opposite of hardness. He did whatever he was told by God. He did all the work according to all which the Lord commanded as to materials, colors, designs and dimensions. Because he did nothing out of his own thought, he was considered the meekest of men.

The story of Moses' building the tabernacle supplies us with many spiritual insights concerning the place we ought to take in spiritual service. Every matter pertaining to the tabernacle was decided by God, who had not left even one item to Moses for decision. He did not permit Moses to follow his own dictum whatsoever. He told the latter not only the framework of the tabernacle but also the details within that framework. He gave direction to the shape, material, color and measurement of every item as well as indicated how each thing should be made—such as, that the curtains must be woven of fine twined linen and that the candlestick must be beaten out of one lump of pure gold. God had not given His servant any ground for personal opinion-making. He knew what He wanted; He did not need any man to be His counselor. He did not permit His servant to do His work according to man's own idea.

The greatest blessing to a servant of Christ is to ar-

rive at the mountain of God's direction, to know
what work is appointed to him, and to be acquainted
with the foreordained pattern of that work. When
you as a servant of Christ come before the Lord and
seek for an appointment, do you come to ask Him to
show you the time and the way of your labor? Or do
you perform the work according to man's counsel,
plan and decision?

Some people seem to think that God has no de-
tailed plan for His work, and that therefore many
things are left to their own opinions. They fail to see
that in the work of God they are but servants to do
what they are commanded. They have not noticed
this word in the Bible: "Whatsoever he saith unto
you, do it" (John 2.5). They forget that they are only
members of Christ's body whose responsibility it is to
"hold fast the head" and to be under the absolute
control of the Head. They imagine that God needs
their natural life and energy to fill up what is lacking
in His counsel.

How you and I really need to ask God for revelation in this respect to enable us to see that in His work
Christ is the absolute Lord. Nothing which pertains to
the work of God must be done without His command. The power of God's servant together with the
fruit of spiritual effectiveness are only to be obtained
and manifested by the servant seeking with uncompli-
cated mind to know the will of God and to undertake
accordingly. Otherwise, however active may be the
work and successful in its appearance, it will be
revealed one day at the judgment seat of Christ to be
but wood, hay and straw in a fire.

Two

"Keep back thy servant also from presumptuous sins; let them not have dominion over me: then shall I be upright, and I shall be clear from great transgression" (Ps. 19.13). From this verse of David's psalm we are shown that there are two kinds of sin before God: one is the sin of rebellion, the other is that of presumption. Not doing what one is told to do constitutes the sin of rebellion. Now we all know the sinfulness of this kind of sin; and from this sin we wish to be delivered. But please take note that besides the sin of rebellion there is also that of presumption, which is, that we do what we are not ordered to do. Rebellion is failing to do what God has charged, whereas presumption is doing what God has not commanded at all. To be active outside of the Lord's will is to be presumptuous. On the one hand God says, Do not commit adultery, Do not steal. If anyone should commit such an act, he is guilty. This we all know. But on the other hand, do we know that it is equally sinful for us to act without God's order? It is reckoned as sin before the Lord if we work for Him without His command and instead work according to our own idea, even though we may view what we do to be most excellent. The prayer of David is for Jehovah to keep him away from presumptuous sin.

God knows what He wants. He therefore tells us, either through the Bible or through the Holy Spirit, what He wishes us to do. For spiritual work depends not on its quantity but on its fitting in to God's purpose and meeting God's use. What matters most to a

servant of Christ is to know what God wants him to
do, and at what time and by what means. One who
serves the Lord has absolutely no need to design his
work. One of the characteristics of the New Covenant
is that everyone may know God's will. A servant of
Christ may receive in his spirit the revelation of the
Holy Spirit, thus discerning clearly what God requires
of him. Such knowledge is real; it comes neither from
his imagination nor from the encouragement or direction of other people. It is based on the teaching of the
letter of the Bible and revealed as God's command in
the deepest recess of his being by the Holy Spirit who
dwells in his spirit.

Yet how many today really know spiritual revelation? How many can truly say, "I have seen it
clearly?" Many there are who substitute for the work
of God that which they deem to be good and spiritual, much to be desired, and calculated to be most
profitable. In the Lord's work there are probably
more volunteers than actually chosen by Him. Many
can only say "I come"; but they cannot say "I am
sent"! Hence a great deal of so-called divine work is
full of death. Numerous are the endeavors which are
not desired by God but are designed by men according to their own zeal and supposition. They call all
these labors works of God, yet in reality they have
almost nothing of God in them.

The prime mover of true spiritual work is the
Lord, not us. We are only made responsible to know
the divine will. Whatever is spiritually effective must
originate from God's heart; we are merely to do what
the Holy Spirit has revealed to us. As a matter of fact,

all services can be traced to either of two sources: one proceeds from God, the other proceeds from man; one is desired by God while the other is what man thinks God may desire. Oh do let us inquire as to what kind of work we have done.

It is most regrettable that many servants of God overlook or little understand this sin of presumption. They have not been brought by the Holy Spirit to the place where they will judge themselves rigorously and acknowledge that in divine work they are not given liberty to voice their opinion because God himself is the sole Lord. How we need the Holy Spirit to convict us of what the sin of presumption is and how terrible is such sin. We should realize that doing what God has *not* charged is as sinful as not doing what He *has* charged us. We must not habitually say, "Since the Lord has not prohibited, why can I not do it?" Rather, we ought frequently to maintain this attitude of heart: "How can I do what God has not charged?" Those who know the Lord only superficially assume that they can do anything which is not prohibited in the Bible; but those who know Him more deeply understand that they would be committing a presumptuous sin if they attempted to do what the Scriptures have not forbidden and yet God has not commanded them to do.

Do recognize this fact, that when you are brought one day to a deeper place with God, you will see that you should not do what He has not ordered just as you must not rebel against what He has ordered. You will be perfect and usable if you do not follow your own thought in things unadvised by God. A perfect man will not commit presumptuous sin. If God has not given an order, such a one will wait in quietness. Such a person is usable and can be used to do the Lord's work.

How often in God's labor people do not ask what His will is, neither do they inquire about His time or way. The best of their attempts are but the labors of their soul life. Let us understand that the flesh may desire to help as well as to resist the Lord. This soul life may stir up zeal for God, conceive ideas for the revival of the church of God, plan for the enlargement of His kingdom, and strive for the winning of many sinners. The motive and intent of these people are good, but they are ignorant as to what the natural life can do in the realm of zeal, planning and striving. They do not perceive that doing what God has ordered is alone commendable; they imagine that the mere doing of His work is something superb. They have yet to realize that whatever comes out of the natural life cannot please God, regardless how pure the motive, how good the aim, or how appealing the result. Because it fails to issue out of God's will, it cannot meet His use. Nor do they realize, in addition, that God will not supply power to any work which is not according to His will. And consequently, they reckon their zeal, voice, emotion, effort and tears to be God-given helps. And hence who among them knows that they are simply drawing on the power of their natural life to supply strength for the work of their own.

What is the cause for presumption? Nothing can account for it but the expression of the self-life.

Though many people are willing to obey when commanded, their hearts take no delight in God's will
because they still like their own idea. Consequently,
they tend to act presumptuously whenever the Lord is
silent. Let me say that unless we judge our flesh and
take up the cross which deals with our self-life, we on
the one hand may perhaps struggle to obey God when
ordered but on the other hand will certainly act with
our own thought if unadvised.

To be presumptuous in the Lord's work does not
necessarily mean to have a wrong intention. Before
we were converted, our self-life did not like to serve
God; but once saved, we do like to serve Him. This,
then, becomes a most dangerous time. For whereas
formerly we absolutely refused to serve the Lord, we
now desire to do so, yet only to serve Him in our own
way. God, however, demands that we not only serve
Him but also serve according to the way He prefers.
How frequently His people are mistaken, thinking
that God only requires service and leaves the way of
service to man's discretion. May we be enlightened to
see that the Lord is not pleased with any service which
is not done in accordance with His will. Moreover, we
should also be assured that both the time and the way
to proceed in the work have likewise been ordained of
the Lord.

We ought to recognize that however correct man's
motive is, it cannot be a substitute for God's will; no
matter how successful a man's endeavor may appear
to be, it can fall short of the divine pleasure. How
many have been the works which were done not in
obedience to the Lord's command but rather in meet-

ing circumstantial needs, in helping believers' spiritual life, or in saving sinners' souls. Such labors may not be fruitless, yet neither the workers nor the works satisfy the Lord's heart. What we must consider first is God's need at the moment, not the outward demands of saints or sinners. The primary objective of our labor is to fulfill *God's* needs, not those of saints and sinners.

Oh do let us see that we are *God's* servants. Though He has entrusted His work to us, He nevertheless reserves for himself the authority to direct His servants. For do recall that at Antioch the Holy Spirit called the Lord's servants to the work, yet Paul and Silas could not go to Asia by their own choice. The authority over the movement of the Lord's servants is forever in the hands of the Holy Spirit (see Acts 16.6ff.). The question lies not in whether there is need in Asia but whether God has a need in Asia *at that particular time.* How marvelously the book of Acts shows that the Holy Spirit who gives us power to work is also the One who sets the direction and timing of our work. Our responsibility in the work is simply to supply God's current need.

The Bible attests to us the fact that we are not hired by God but are bought with Jesus' blood. And because of this, He has absolute authority over us and therefore we cannot follow our own will. God has not assigned any work to us for us then to decide how best it should be done. No, He has a specific order for each work. He neither will be pleased nor will use us if we presuppose anything without His definite command. All such works cannot stand the fire but will instead be burned up.

Finally, it should be noted that the Bible also affirms that God manifests His glory not only in the large but also in the small things. We therefore ought to let Him have preeminence in all things. We should exalt Him as the Lord of little matters as well as of big matters. He is through all and in all. If what we do is not according to His will, we may be praised by men but certainly not approved by God.

Three

The Bible illustrates this principle of which we have been speaking with many instances. Consider, for instance, *Nadab and Abihu*.

> And Nadab and Abihu, the sons of Aaron, took each of them his censer, and put fire therein, and laid incense thereon, and offered strange fire before Jehovah, which he had not commanded them. And there came forth fire from before Jehovah, and devoured them, and they died before Jehovah. (Lev. 10.1–2)

The law of incense burning demands that each time incense is burned it must be kindled by the fire on the altar. The failure of Nadab and Abihu lay in using strange or alien fire rather than the altar fire; consequently they were burned to death in God's presence.

The altar is a type of the cross. Incense represents

our service before God. The zeal for our service must come from the altar or the cross. Whoever does not follow this law will die. What is the cross? It is where our self-life is put to death; it also is where we let the Lord live. This agrees with Galatians 2: "I have been crucified with Christ; and it is no longer I that live, but Christ liveth in me" (v.20). The cross deals with the wisdom, opinion, strength, zeal, expectation and desire of our self-life. Only after we have passed through such dealings are we fit to come before God and serve.

Who knows how much of our zeal is strange fire! Ofttimes people conjecture over how to prosper the Lord's work and to please God: such conjecturing is all according to their fleshly thoughts without themselves having been dealt with by the cross or having had their cleverness denied. Zeal yes, but not of God. It indeed is fire, but it is foreign fire instead of altar fire. Whatever does not come from the cross, that is to say, from the self-denying altar, is merely strange fire. Such fire is nothing but "self-fire"—that which proceeds from the soul life. It is the fire and power of the natural life. And hence it is the self-life intervening in God's affairs. The affair may unquestionably belong to God, nonetheless self-life decides how it is to be done. If we depend on our wisdom, use our method, or insist on our opinion in the Lord's affairs, we are offering strange fire—fire which is not only unacceptable to God but even causes our death in His presence.

Nadab and Abihu were Aaron's sons, and Aaron was God's chosen high priest. What these two men did was not rebellious against God, for their intent was to burn incense to serve and to please Him. Yet what they did was what He had not commanded. Because they failed to be conformed to God's appointed way, they were judged by Him. These two sons of Aaron thought that since God had not prohibited the use of other fire in kindling incense, then unusual fire could be used; but they did not realize that in God's service whatever is not specifically ordered by Him is not to be done by His servants. They were blind to the strictness of God. In the service of the Lord, that which He has not commanded is forbidden. It is wrong and sinful to do such a thing. God consumed Nadab and Abihu with fire because they committed the sin of presumption. He did not spare them, even though they were Aaron's sons appointed to be priests.

They had not committed adultery or robbery, like the priestly sons of Eli; nor did they rebel against God's clear command in doing what was forbidden. They especially wished to serve the Lord and to please Him. Hence they took their respective censers and put strange fire on the incense, thinking that they would obtain the Lord's pleasure by doing so. Though their intention was good, they nonetheless served God according to their own idea. They performed what He had not charged; they did something outside His will. And such action offended Him. In serving the Lord we should not take for granted that our good intention is His will. Our intention may be good, but if it is done presumptuously we will be punished for our presumptuous sin. Perhaps in our labors today we may not for the moment see God's severe judgment, nevertheless all the works of alien fire shall be manifested and judged at the judgment seat of Christ in the future.

May God open our eyes to perceive what sin is. There is no doubt that adultery, robbery, distortion, unrighteousness, and uncleanness are sins, but to do the Lord's work, or to preach, help others, and so forth without the divine command are actions which are also sinful. God will judge such presumptuous sins. Whatever is done without His order is serving with strange fire and is abominable to Him.

Saul's offering the burnt-offering as recorded in 1 Samuel 13.8–14 may also serve as a great warning to us. He offered the sacrifice himself for at least three reasons: first, he saw that the people were scattered from him; second, Samuel had not come at the appointed time; and third, the Philistines assembled themselves at Michmash ready to attack him at Gilgal. For these reasons, he *forced* himself to sacrifice the burnt-offering. Here Saul had not committed anything evil, for he offered a sacrifice to the Lord. He thought in his heart, How could he receive the needed favor of the Lord without prayer? He concluded that if he prayed more, he would be favored— that if he performed a little more service towards the Lord, he would be empowered to deliver his people from the enemy's hands. What a surprise it must have been to Saul for Samuel to have said to him:

Thou hast done foolishly; thou hast not kept the

commandment of Jehovah thy God, which he commanded thee: for now would Jehovah have established thy kingdom upon Israel forever. But now thy kingdom shall not continue: Jehovah hath sought him a man after his own heart, and Jehovah hath appointed him to be prince over his people, because thou hast not kept that which Jehovah commanded thee. (1 Sam. 13.13–14)

Saul's "therefore said I" (v.12) was not God's command. From this we may learn that God wishes us to serve Him according to His command, not according to what we think or suppose. Whatever work is based on what we assume or devise is rejected by the Lord. For He looks for a man after His own heart. He values what we obey more than what we do: "Behold, to obey is better than sacrifice, and to hearken than the fat of rams" (1 Sam. 15.22). This ought to be remembered by every servant of God.

How very often we hasten to do things just as Saul did. We cannot believe that God is *never* late; we are not able to wait for His time. We only see our need and circumstance, and neglect to wait for the divine time. And thus we do that which the Lord has not ordered.

We know Saul was rejected by God because he was too zealous, too eager to offer sacrifice, too hasty in prayer. How manifold were his reasons for action; nevertheless, God in the meantime had sought for himself a man after His own heart and had appointed him to be prince over His people. The man the Lord desires is not one who is so hasty that he cannot wait. If the choice were left to us, we would undoubtedly incline towards people like Saul; for was he not an unusual man? He stood head and shoulders above all the people. Yet God does not seek for an unusual man, but a man after His own heart. May the aim of our service to the Lord not be so much a desiring to do great things so that we as well as others may be pleased, but may it be a touching of the heart of God in order that He may be delighted. Only people such as this will God use. He is looking for such men.

David and the ark. Let us pursue this subject further by inquiring once again into 2 Samuel 6.1-7:

> And David again gathered together all the chosen men of Israel, thirty thousand. And David arose, and went with all the people that were with him, from Baal-e-judah, to bring up from thence the ark of God, which is called by the Name, even the name of Jehovah of hosts that sitteth above the cherubim. And they set the ark of God upon a new cart, and brought it out of the house of Abinadab that was in the hill: and Uzzah and Ahio, the sons of Abinadab, drove the new cart. And they brought it out of the house of Abinadab, which was in the hill, with the ark of God: and Ahio went before the ark. . . . And when they came to the threshing-floor of Nacon, Uzzah put forth his hand to the ark of God, and took hold of it; for the oxen stumbled. And the anger of Jehovah was kindled against Uzzah; and God smote him there for his error; and there he died by the ark of God.

We have discussed this incident earlier, but in reading this passage once more many may now ask again why Uzzah was smitten. Should not his steadying of the ark with his outstretched hand be viewed as meritorious? Was not the glory of God involved with the ark; and that therefore in holding the ark steady, had not Uzzah performed a great service? Why then did God immediately strike him to death? It is for no other reason than that the Lord wants people to obey His command more than to help in His work. The Lord does not need any man to uphold His glory. Whoever touches the ark of God's presence must die. And hence the question here lies not so much in the effect which would occur were the ark to fall as in the fact of man doing what God has not ordered. It is quite natural for man to conclude that even if in peaceful time the ark should never be touched, in time of danger it *could* be touched and held lest it topple over—for this is an emergency measure which ought to be accepted without the penalty of death. Yet God has only one rule; He does not believe in compromise. Whoever does anything without His order is subject to death—and if not physical, then spiritual.

God does not ask here whether you and I have done good or bad, nor does He inquire if we have helped Him. He only declares that our hands should not touch the ark, for whoever does must die. He would rather have the ark fall down; He does not like anyone to help Him without His command. Yet how often we think of helping the Lord when we are faced with external need. But is it not terrible that God's servants tend to use fleshly hands in helping Him just as Uzzah did? Can they be exempt from His judgment? Let us be advised that all we need to watch out for is the commandment of God. Whatever is done as an emergency against circumstantial need without waiting for the divine command is unacceptable to Him. We may permit our work to fail temporarily (in appearance at least), but God's sovereignty must not for one moment be trespassed nor can man's flesh at any time be released. God has no need for the flesh to help in His work; and He will most surely judge all fleshly activities.

While we were yet sinners we lived and worked according to our own wisdom, thus doing many things against God's nature. And now that we are saved, we think we can still use our wisdom to serve and help God according to our best judgment—little realizing that using our wisdom to help in the Lord's work after we are saved is as sinful and unacceptable as using our wisdom to oppose Him while we were sinners. The Lord has no need for the help of our wisdom. He dislikes the assistance of unrenewed human wisdom as much as the opposition of the same wisdom. For this reason, therefore, we should accept the rule of the cross in denying all the activities of the self-life by willingly putting the flesh to death and truly forfeiting our own opinion. Whenever in the Lord's work we do things according to our own idea, we demonstrate the lack of self-denial and of the experiential knowledge of the cross. We must be brought to zero, otherwise we cannot be used by God.

May we not be presumptuous and interfere with the Lord's work. Even if a work is going to fall we cannot hold it with the hand of the flesh, because we can only do what the Lord wants us to do. God does not hold us responsible for what He has not ordered. He will not reprimand us even if such work falls apart at our side.

As a matter of fact, however, all presumptuous acts are committed through a lack of the dealing of the cross with man's wisdom. What the Lord requires of us today, and to which we should hold fast, is simply this: that what God has commanded we will do; what He has not commanded we will not do. We ought to keep within our place.

Some may deem this way to be too narrow; for, they ask, will not their work be too common if they should follow this rule? But one day they will know whether or not this way is the right one. In that day, they will be shown that all the works outside God's will are bad and worthless. Whatever is done outside the divine will will not escape reproach at the judgment seat of Christ.

King Uzziah. We are told in 2 Chronicles 26.16–21 how King Uzziah was punished by God when he intended to burn incense upon the altar of incense in the temple of the Lord. God's design was that only the sons of Aaron who were consecrated to the priesthood could enter the temple to burn incense and that none else was allowed to perform this duty. But Uzziah's heart was so lifted up as to insist on his burning incense in the temple. Leprosy appeared instantly on his brow as the result of God's punishment. This incident serves as a further warning to us that we should never act presumptuously without the divine command lest we too be punished. Leprosy in the spiritual

sense signifies a sin of defilement. Whoever under-
takes anything without the Lord's command commits
before God the sin of defilement. In divine work,
therefore, man's own zeal is useless, because he is not
allowed to direct the work by his zealousness. It is an
excellent thing to enter the temple to burn incense;
such action, however, becomes a sin to be punished if
it is not ordered by God. King Uzziah offended the
Lord by presumptuously entering the temple to burn
incense; with the result that he became a leper and remained so till the day of his death. We cannot ignore
such an extraordinary warning.

Four

Paul is an apostle of deep spirituality. Please notice what he wrote to the saints at Corinth in his second letter:

> But we will not glory beyond our measure, but
> according to the measure of the province which
> God apportioned to us as a measure, to reach even
> unto you: . . . but having hope that, as your
> faith groweth, we shall be magnified in you ac-
> cording to our province unto further abundance.
> (10.13–15)

Paul here speaks out of his experience. He says he
will not overextend himself beyond the measure of the
sphere which God has apportioned to him. He will
not go to wherever the Lord has not measured it out
to him. He senses his responsibility in what God holds

him responsible; but he dare not be responsible over that which God has not entrusted to him. How could the church ever have strife or division in such a matter if all God's servants were to keep this rule? Each servant of the Lord has a measure of the sphere of work which God has apportioned to him; each believer has a divinely-appointed course to finish. If each one will stand in his post, do his share of work, and finish his appointed course, what a glory shall be seen!

In divine service let us not be governed by our seeing that the work is good, that it may save souls, or that it helps people. Rather let us see whether our task is within the measure of the sphere which heaven apportions to us. A huge pillar is certainly essential to a house, but a small nail is not any the less needed. How can the church be established if each one in the church aspires to be a great revivalist or a great evangelist or a great teacher? Ought we not walk in the course of the Lord's will? We should not aim at a great thing; we should stand instead in the place of God's choice. If He wants us to do a small work quietly, we are happy to do it. For God does not seek "great talent"; He uses whoever is usable. May we be willing to take our place under the divine appointment. Let me say frankly that we must guard against all pretensions and ambitions, for these aspirations are worldly, soulish and carnal. And once we understand this, we will never dare touch the work of God lightly.

"I have finished the course," declared Paul (2 Tim. 4.7). What is this course to which the apostle refers? Mrs. Jessie Penn-Lewis, in her autobiographical sketch, made the following remarks:

> There is a "course" prepared for each believer from the moment of his new birth, providing for the fullest maturity of the new life within him, and the highest which God can make of his life in the use of every faculty for His service. To discover that "course" and fulfill it is the one duty of every soul. Others cannot judge what that course is. God alone knows it, and He can make it known, and guide the believer into it, as certainly today as He did in the day of Jeremiah and other prophets, and of Paul and Philip and other apostles.*

A glorious thing for a child of God is to be able to stand in the place of the Lord's choice and do the work of His appointment. For the Lord has preordained a course for each believer to finish.

God always uses His *chosen* ones to do His work; He does not need volunteers for His task. Whoever is chosen by Him has absolutely no liberty. If any of His chosen ones desires the freedom to walk in his own way, he will experience nothing but failure and pain. Yet if anyone is at all chosen, he will not be able to flee from God's appointed course. Even if he should flee to Tarshish (as did the prophet Jonah), he will be thrown into the sea and brought back by a great fish. There is no escape for such a one. A servant of God must never do anything according to his own will or

---

*An extract from an autobiograhical sketch written by Mrs. Penn-Lewis for *The Overcomer* Magazine in one of its 1914 issues.—*Author*

conception, because the man whom the Lord selects is one who will only do the work which God has apportioned to him and run the course which God has prepared.

When Moses brought the Israelites through the wilderness he was commanded by the Lord to warn the people not to work on the sabbath. However, he made no immediate move to deal with the man who was found gathering sticks on the sabbath day because he had not yet received any instruction from God. It was only after the Lord had clearly said to Moses—"the man shall surely be put to death"—that the congregation stoned him to death (Num. 15.32-36). Moses waited for God to tell him what to do before he dared to do anything. He dared not offer his own opinion.

God's work will be greatly damaged if we are not willing to wait a while. How hasty is our nature. We always feel that the Lord is too slow. We are not able to follow His guidance step by step. We hasten to do what we consider to be good. We unhesitatingly supply where we find something is lacking. We are afraid we may waste our entire life and do nothing if we pause for anything. We forget how blessed are those who can wait before God and then do His bidding.

Five

A great responsibility which we have before the Lord is this: that we need to be absolutely clear concerning His command before we do His work. We must not attempt anything without having His order

first. God's command expresses what His heart de
sires. If we wish to be useful vessels in His hand, we
must never move unless we receive His command. For
we will not please Him if we perform the work which
He has not charged us to do. Whenever a piece of
work is laid before us, our first concern should be
whether this is according to His will and is acceptable
to His heart. May we only seek to be conformed to
His will.

In summary, then, the pattern which God shows
on the mount should never be altered according to
man's idea. On the contrary, it must be closely followed. If it is *our* work, we need not do it according
to God's will; but if it is *God's* work, then we must
follow His will. Who can refrain from sighing that
frequently God's work is spoiled in man's fleshly
hand! Let us therefore keep well in mind that unless
our wisdom is judged and our thoughts are delivered
to death, we cannot perform divine work. May we be
brought to know nothing but God's will, without self
or self-opinion. Each time we do a work, we first ask
what is the Lord's will. And after we know for certain
His will, let us do it according to His revealed pattern.

PART TWO

"RECKONED AS FAITHFUL"

1 | The Book of Acts Goes On

And Paul abode two whole years in his own hired dwelling, and received all that went in unto him, preaching the kingdom of God, and teaching the things concerning the Lord Jesus Christ with all boldness, none forbidding him. (Acts 28.30–31)

Saying, What thou seest, write in a book and send it to the seven churches: unto Ephesus, and unto Smyrna, and unto Pergamum, and unto Thyatira, and unto Sardis, and unto Philadelphia, and unto Laodicea. And I turned to see the voice that spake with me. And having turned I saw seven golden candlesticks; . . The mystery of the seven stars which thou sawest in my right hand, and the seven golden candlesticks. The seven stars are the angels of the seven churches: and the seven candlesticks are seven churches. (Rev. 1.11–12,20)

The Bible is a composite of 66 books. Of these 66, many—with respect to their subject matter—are obviously concluded at the end of their reading. For example, the book of Genesis has 50 chapters. When you read to the very last chapter, you instinctively feel that that is the end. Matthew has 28 chapters and you sense quite naturally when you come to its final chapter that it is truly the end. The same feeling comes to you after you have read Romans chapter 16 or Revelation chapter 22.

But there is one very special book in the Bible about which you could not say you have reached the end. You can say that it is the end of the matter with regard to many of the other 65 books of the Bible, but about this particular book you cannot. And that is the book of Acts. When you arrive at chapter 28, you are surprised that it should close so abruptly. You really sense it is not yet concluded. And as a matter of historical fact, this book of Acts truly has no end, because what it speaks about is indeed still going on. The record of the acts of the apostles of the first century may be concluded, but the record of the apostles of all succeeding centuries has not been completed. Up to the present moment, in fact, you continue to read about the acts of God's apostles. In short, the book of Acts has not yet been finished.

"My Father worketh even until now," declared the Lord, "and I work" (John 5.17). This tells us the fact that ever since the rebellion of Satan and the fall of man God has been working until now, and so also has the Son been at work. How about what we find in the Acts? Let me say that the book of Acts is not a record of the work of Paul nor of the work of Peter; it is the record of the work of God. Who can say that after the time of Acts 28 God labors no more? Who can dare say that the work of the Lord comes to an end at Acts 28?

This book has no conclusion. After the period of chapter 28, God still has many vessels who do His work. The labor of the Lord continues on; it does not stop there. Paul's life did not end after his two years' work in Rome. So far as his entire life is concerned, after his stay in Rome for those two years, he was released from prison and was able to visit new places as well as some old ones. He was later taken captive and was finally martyred. These events were not set down in the book of Acts. We need to note that Peter and Paul and John were three important persons in the church of God, yet none of their concluding periods of life was ever recorded fully in the Scriptures. Can we accurately say, then, that the book of Acts is ended?

How can the testimony of God ever be fully written? It is truly without end. Neither a chapter 29 nor a chapter 30 nor even up to a 100th chapter will or can ever be written. New things would need to be added on all the time if the writing were to go on. For this reason, therefore, Acts must stop abruptly at chapter 28. Nevertheless, though nothing is further recorded after that chapter, the work of God has continued onward. The work of the first century did not reach its zenith. If the work that God has accomplished during these 4,000 years were to be consummated at the end of an Acts 28, then we would now be at the bottom of the mountain and God's work would have by now greatly declined. But nothing of this sort has happened. For the Lord plainly declares, "My Father worketh even until now, and I work."

Let us not assume that the work of God reached its zenith at the time of Paul or at the time of Martin Luther. The first century did not conclude God's work, and neither did the sixteenth century terminate His work. The Lord's work shall proceed forth until the kingdom age, and even to the new heaven and the new earth will it still go on without end. And if we believe as well as know this truth, we shall praise God.

People often commit this error: they think that they live in the worst period of the church. People at the time of Martin Luther thought so; people at the time of John Wesley also thought this. We would say, however, that the era of Martin Luther was very good, and that the period of John Wesley was likewise very good. Perhaps fifty years from now, people will even say that the time we live in today was good. We are fearful lest men stop working, but let us understand that God will never cease working. Each year He knows what He will do. Each year He knows how far He will go. Each year He will accomplish what He has purposed to do. Daily will God go on; He always advances. Hallelujah, the Lord continually moves forward!

We must see that whenever God moves forward He always has His vessels. In the period of the book of Acts, He had His vessels. At the time of Martin Luther, He had His vessels. And during the time of John Wesley, He likewise had His vessels. In each period of spiritual revival, God has had His own vessels. Where, then, it should be asked, are God's vessels today? Unquestionably the Father works until now, but who among men continue to cooperate with Him? Who will say, as did the Lord Jesus, "and I work"? This becomes a serious question.

If at this point we are given a little light by God so as to see a little of His reality, we shall come to acknowledge that the vessel which God today seeks for is the very one which He in the beginning has always had in mind—which is His church. In other words, the vessel which God ultimately looks for today is not an individual one, rather it is corporate in nature. And if He indeed needs a corporate vessel today, we will immediately realize that unless His children are brought to see what is the body of Christ and what is body life, they will be useless in the Lord's work and will not be able to arrive at God's aim.

The first chapter of Revelation tells us that the church is the golden candlestick. God in His word not only says the church is golden, He also says that the church is the golden candlestick. If the church is only golden, she cannot satisfy God's heart. Why does God say the church is the golden *candlestick*? Because the golden candlestick serves the purpose of spreading the light so that the light may shine far and wide. God wants the church to be a shining vessel, a vessel of testimony. From the very beginning He has ordained the church to be a candlestick. Not one certain person, but the entire church. In the divine view the church is a candlestick. It is therefore not enough for it simply to be golden, which means that everything about it is of God: it must also shine for God and testify for Him as the golden candlestick.

The church exists for the testimony of God. If it is not golden, it is not the church. Yet if it is not also a candlestick, it is still not the church. If there be no life within, it cannot be the church; but then, too, if there be no testimony within, it will not be the church either. The church must understand what God expects to do and to obtain in this age. She will be a golden candlestick if she sees what the testimony of God on earth is today.

May we reiterate quite simply here, that the work of God proceeds onward, that the Lord still looks for the suitable vessel, and that His vessel today is the same as that which was true at the beginning—which is to say, that it is not something individual but something collective in nature: in other words, the church.

People will perhaps ask concerning the overcomers in the church. True, the church is in great need of overcomers; but the testimony of these overcomers is for the benefit of the corporate entity, not for that of the personal. Overcomers are not a class of people who deem themselves to be superior, esteeming themselves as better than the others and pushing them aside. Not so. They instead work for the entire body. They do the work, and the whole church receives the benefit. Overcomers are not for themselves; rather, they stand on the ground of the church and bring it to maturity. Hence the victory of the overcomers becomes also the victory of the whole church.

Now since the vessel God needs is a corporate one, we must learn to live the body life. And to live out body life we must deny our natural life. We must receive deep dealings from God. Being dealt with by Him and having learned obedience and fellowship, we may have the privilege of being His vessel.

2 | Run the Race Set before Us

Therefore, let us also, seeing we are compassed about with so great a cloud of witnesses, lay aside every weight, and the sin which doth so easily beset us, and let us run with patience the race that is set before us, looking unto Jesus the author and perfecter of our faith, who for the joy that was set before him endured the cross, despising shame, and hath sat down at the right hand of the throne of God. For consider him that hath endured such gainsaying of sinners against himself, that ye wax not weary, fainting in your souls. (Heb. 12.1–3)

One

God places two considerations before men: first, He presents eternal life to sinners; and second, He presents the kingdom to all who already have eternal life. All who believe have eternal life; nevertheless, as Jesus said to His believing disciples, "Except your righteousness shall exceed the righteousness of the scribes and Pharisees, ye shall in no wise enter into the kingdom of heaven'' (Matt. 5.20). The Lord Jesus also declared this: ''Not every one that saith unto me, Lord, Lord, shall enter into the kingdom of heaven; but he that doeth the will of my Father who is in heaven'' (Matt. 7.21). Thus we are shown that to have eternal life one need only believe, but to enter the kingdom one is required to fulfill another condition.

Soon after a person is saved he is set by God on a specific course that lies ahead of him. The entire life of a Christian can be likened to running a race. Yet this is not a racing towards the goal of eternal life. It does not mean that he who wins this race will have as his prize eternal life; on the contrary, only the person who has eternal life is qualified to run. No, the result of this race is that some of the participants are to be crowned while others will not be (see 1 Cor. 9.24–25).

What is meant by the crown? The crown represents the kingdom. It signifies reigning, having dominion and glory. And thus to obtain the crown means to gain the kingdom—that is to say, to reign with the Lord Jesus and to have dominion and glory. And to lose the crown means to not have the kingdom —a not reigning with the Lord nor receiving dominion and glory. Hence the crown is the symbol of the kingdom. For a Christian, having eternal life is already a settled matter, but having the kingdom depends on how that Christian runs.

As soon as a person is saved he is set by God on a course which leads straight to the kingdom. His words, his conduct, his thoughts, his life—in fact his everything—is related to whether or not he may gain the kingdom. Now the believer who refuses to run the race judges himself as being unfit for the kingdom; and the believer who runs poorly jeopardizes his chances of winning the kingdom. Now God has already placed every Christian on this course. Yet whether or not he shall win the kingdom is a matter that can only be decided by his own self. His consecration, faithfulness and victory will help him to receive the crown. But for those who love the world and follow after the flesh, they shall not gain the kingdom of the heavens—even though they are the possessors of eternal life by having trusted in the Lord Jesus.

Two

To whom do these "witnesses" in Hebrews 12.1 have reference? They seem to point to those men of great faith cited previously in chapter 11; but actually they refer not to those men but to the things done by them. For the word "witness" is the same term used in Acts 1.8, 1.22, 2.32, and so forth, and hence it can also be interpreted as referring to the things to which they witness. What the word of God says here is that the witnesses given to the things done by these men of faith surround us as a cloud.

What do these witnesses intend to prove? They prove the "so great a salvation" of God (Heb. 2.3–4). This great salvation alludes not to the forgiveness of sins but points instead to the kingdom. For the kingdom is the goal of our running the race. God gives us so many witnesses in order to encourage us to live the life of faith, to run the race, and to win the glory of the kingdom. Though what the great men of faith mentioned in chapter 11 believe may not be directly linked to the kingdom, nonetheless, their faith being their course, they keep on believing in spite of everything—that is to say, they leave all to finish their course. They have received what they believe directly, such as that some are raptured, some are resurrected, some obtain the land, and some are saved from perishing. Still these are not the ultimate which God has promised to give them. What they have received through faith are but demonstrations to assure them of obtaining the promised kingdom: "And these all, having had witness borne to them through their faith, received not the promise, God having provided some better thing concerning us, that apart from us they should not be made perfect" (Heb. 11.39–40). What is the promise referred to here? None other than the kingdom: those people have already had the witness borne to them that God will give them the kingdom.

"So great a cloud of witnesses"—Because of their faith God has given them grace. He has answered prayers and performed miracles, thus proving that He is pleased with their running their course and will assuredly give them the kingdom. Our being surrounded by so great a cloud of witnesses, let us too run the course of faith.

God has placed the kingdom before us; He has set a course for us to run. At the finish, failure or success will be seen. He who overcomes shall reign with

Christ; but he who is defeated, and even though he is saved, shall have no part in the kingdom's glory.

Three

The course is now set; and consequently, the runners must "lay aside every weight, and the sin which doth so easily beset us . . . " In running, two matters are absolutely important: the one is to lay aside every weight, and the other is to put away sin.

Let us talk about putting away sin first. Sin hinders progress the most. It disqualifies people from running. Sin is the trespassing of the rules; and he who would trespass the rules is not allowed to run a race. He is ordered to the sidelines.

A believer ought to put off and forsake the sin which he knows. Be it jealousy, pride, uncleanness of heart, lies in the mouth, hasty temper, or unrestrained lust—it will make him unfit for the race. He who has lost the privilege of running the race loses the possibility of entering the kingdom and reigning with Christ. A Christian must stand on Romans 6.6 and 6.11 and reckon himself as dead to sin. He must forsake sins and must not allow sin to reign over him. He must also yield his members as instruments of righteousness to God. Whatever offends the Lord must be honestly confessed, repented of, and forsaken so as to obtain God's forgiveness.

No one with an evil conscience can run the race which is set before him. We should not retain any unforsaken sin lest we harbor a lasting uneasy conscience. If we have sinned against anyone we ought to

apologize in good faith. If we have defrauded anybody we must make restitution to the best of our ability. There should not be any wrong towards anybody
that is not cleared up. Do not be afraid of incurring
loss, nor be fearful of losing face. Or else you will not
be able to run this race. We need to pay special attention to certain sins which do not appear to be as ugly
as we think. For these are the sins which can so easily
beset us. It is said of Moses that he "[chose] rather to
share ill-treatment with the people of God, than to
enjoy the pleasures of sin for a season" (Heb. 11.25).
This plainly indicates that sin does have its pleasures.
Many sins give pleasure to people. The human flesh
delights to sin because sin provides its pleasure. But
he who truly has faith would rather suffer persecution
and reproach than to enjoy the pleasure of sin. We
ought to resist sin, otherwise we judge ourselves as
unfit for the kingdom.

Let us turn now to the matter of "laying aside
every weight." What is a weight? A weight may not
be sin, nor is it necessarily something very bad, but it
doubtless can easily entangle us. Our not putting
away sin will disqualify us from ever running the race;
yet our not laying aside every weight, though it will
not keep us from running, will certainly hinder us
from running fast. When would we ever see anyone
running a race with his fur coat on? Anything which
keeps us from running well or hinders our progress
may be viewed as a weight.

During the nineteenth century there was a man
who was greatly used by the Lord. He spent a great
deal of time compiling a Hebrew dictionary. Upon

finishing the work he sent it to his friends for review. All of them praised the work highly. They agreed that once this book was published, he would instantly become a famous scholar. Yet this brother burned his manuscript. For, when he was compiling it, said the would-be scholar, he felt his love for the Lord as well as his love for souls had been greatly diminished. So that for him, to proofread and to print it would subsequently occupy even more of his time and energy. And hence it was better, he concluded, to have it burned. Now to proofread and later to print a manuscript would be no sin, yet for him it would constitute a serious weight. Accordingly, by taking the action he did take, this believer was delivered from a weight.

There are things in your life which may not be termed sinful, yet can they not be viewed as weights to you? Suppose you are to run a race and someone asks you to eat a large bowl of noodles or to be clothed with a heavy fur coat. Do you think you can run in such a condition? Let us see that we must lay aside every weight as well as put off sins. We cannot run well with unnecessary weights on us.

The failure of Lot lay in the area of weight. Lot was not a bad person; on the contrary, twice the apostle called him a righteous man who was "sore distressed by the lascivious life of the wicked" (2 Peter 2.7–8). Yet his life was so different from that of Abraham. The latter lived in the wilderness, but Lot dwelt in the city. Abraham lived in tents, whereas Lot dwelt in a house. Here was to be found their vast difference—that whereas the one was light the other had too many weights. Although Lot could still run even with certain weights, he nevertheless ran his life's race poorly—so much so that he finally gave up running the race and was defeated.

How we need to take heed to the words in Mark 4. In that passage the Lord is not found saying that there is no fruit in a life because of sin but because of weights—for He says there that "the cares of the world, and the deceitfulness of riches, and the lusts of other things entering in, choke the word, and it becometh unfruitful" (v.19). Even one of the many cares of the world (and not necessarily any sin) may cause one to be unfruitful. For example, though riches are no sin, they nevertheless can hinder us in flying as with two wings. Those who desire to be rich cannot run well. And even in the matter of duties which God has apportioned to us, we must faithfully perform; however, if our heart gets entangled with any of them, we shall run with great difficulty.

Let me repeat that weight is not necessarily sin. Many a time a weight can be viewed as quite legitimate. It is nevertheless a weight that decelerates the speed of one's advance. One's weight may be a deeply attached friend, a sought-for position, a bit of worldly ambition, a much desired dwelling, a bowl of delicious food, or a gorgeous piece of apparel. These and many other things may not be sins, yet they all are able to slow down one's speed.

For this reason, we ought to ask ourselves if there is any sin which keeps us from running or if there is any weight which slows down our pace. Sin disqualifies a person from running altogether—that is to say, it takes one out of the race. Weight, on the other hand, keeps a person from running *well* and consumes his strength unprofitably. Let me ask, What is the sin which especially besets you? What is your special weight? Let us carefully search these matters out and quickly lay them aside.

Four

We who are running this race must not only lay aside the sin which easily besets us and also every unnecessary weight but also run this race "with patience." Why with patience? Because the reward is not given at the start, nor in the middle, but at the very end of the course. It is presented after the last step of the race has been taken. You may run well at the beginning, even in the middle period, but you may not run well at the very end.

To win at both the start, the middle, and the end of a race is what is accounted as winning. Before the end is reached, none can guarantee whether he will be rewarded. One may fail at the last five steps. Once in a 200 meters dash, one man ran ahead of the rest by the distance of about twenty meters through most of the race, but then suddenly fell down with only two meters left to the end. In order to win, a person must be very careful. Before the end is reached no one can boast that he has the reward. Even the apostle Paul must say this: "Not that I have already obtained, or am already made perfect: but I press on" (Phil. 3.12). If such was true of Paul, then what about us?

What is meant by the word "run" in the phrase "run with patience the race"? Running is not stand-

ing, nor is it walking slowly. To run is to advance with
speed. Running is using the minimum time to cover
the maximum distance. One therefore has to run fast.
Due to the many participants in the race, a person
must run ahead if he is to win the crown. Whether a
person wins or fails depends on how fast or how
slowly he runs. If he wastes his time and wanders
aimlessly from the course, he is doomed to fail.

This passage in Hebrews 12.1–3 also says that we
run "the race that is set before us"—thus signifying
that there is only one way, and that is the course
which is set before us. We cannot choose the path we
ourselves prefer; we must run the race which God
himself has set before us. Who in an athletic game
would dare to step out of the line drawn in such a
race? All must run within the assigned lines. And such
is the meaning of 2 Timothy 2 which states that "if
. . . a man contend in the games, he is not crowned,
except he have contended lawfully" (v.5)—that is to
say, according to the rules. How very pitiful that
many Christians run zealously, yet they do not run according to the course *God* has set. Our own zeal,
labor and activity cannot substitute for God's rule
and will. Running outside the will of God leads to
loss. Since the Lord has set the course before us, we
must run in it before we may expect to win the
reward.

Five

Our feet need to run according to the lines apportioned to us by God, but in addition, our eyes must

"look unto Jesus the author and perfecter of our faith" (Heb. 12.2a). According to the original, it may be translated as "looking away unto Jesus"— meaning that we are to look away from all the other things around us and look only to Jesus. We do not look at anything but Jesus only. By looking to Him we may run the straight path. There are many things around us which may easily affect our attention and divert us from our goal. Only by looking away to Jesus will we be kept running in God's course.

Christ Jesus is said to be the author and perfecter of our faith. Our faith originates in Him and also concludes in Him. What we believe is He alone. Once we are in the Lord we must always abide in the Lord. We ought to set our mind on Him only. Neither holiness, nor victory, nor perfect love, nor baptism with the Holy Spirit, nor zeal in winning souls, nor any spiritual conflict should steal our heart away from Him. From the beginning to the end, it is the Lord Jesus himself. Our faith takes Him as the end as well as the beginning. Aside from Him we look at nothing. Naturally, if we do continually look off to the Lord Jesus, then holiness, victory, and all the rest of these things will indeed be manifested in our lives. But if we should seek after anything outside of Christ, that thing will make our path crooked. In the course of spiritual pursuit we need to ask God to show us by revelation that *all* things are in *Christ* alone. Forgiveness, justification and regeneration are in Christ. Holiness, victory and fullness of the Holy Spirit are likewise in Christ. Christ is everything. He is the Beginning of all beginnings, the End of all ends. In short, our all is in Him. Apart from the Lord we cannot run the race which is set before us.

"Looking away" is the prerequisite for looking to the Lord. Unless we look away from something, we will not look at Jesus. If one who is running should look here and there, he will not be able to run well. He may even run the wrong way, a crooked way, or even come to a complete stop. Hence God calls us not to look at anything but the Lord Jesus. Furthermore, even recollection within us is harmful to our spiritual pursuit. To recollect concerning oneself, to analyze one's own feelings, to be mindful always of one's progress, or to be overly concerned with one's spiritual condition may all hinder our advance. One of the greatest dangers in running the race is to be overly anxious about our progress, and thus we fall unknowingly into self-recollection and fail to look away to Jesus.

What is then meant by looking to Jesus? It is not to look at one's self. To look off to Jesus is to be so attracted by Him that a person leaves his own inner world and is joined to the One to whom he looks. What kind of Jesus do you look to? You look to a Jesus who is both author and perfecter of your faith —the all-inclusive Jesus. The secret of spiritual advance, then, is to know how not to dwell on one's personal condition. He who knows how not to look at himself is truly blessed. May the Spirit of God give us revelation, causing us to know what "looking away" is and how not to have an improper recollection of oneself.

Six

All this that we have noted now brings us to look at how the Lord Jesus himself ran the race: "Who for the joy that was set before him, endured the cross, despising shame, and hath sat down at the right hand of the throne of God" (Heb. 12.2b). The Lord Jesus looked at the joy that was set before Him and ran straight towards it. What is the joy? Did not He himself say, "Well done, good and faithful servant: . . . enter thou into the joy of thy lord" (Matt. 25.21)? This points to the joy in the millennium. True, our Lord obeyed God His Father according to His inherent nature. But in the Bible we find another fact, which is, that God's reward and promise—especially that of the kingdom—definitely had some influence on Jesus' life. Because of the joy that was set before Him, our Lord Jesus in His earthly race pressed onward bearing both shame and the cross.

Why is it that in the preceding word the writer of this Hebrews passage employs the name "Jesus" and not "Christ" or "the Lord Jesus" (which is His title after resurrection) to identify the author and perfecter of our faith? We know that "Jesus" is the Lord's name as a man. God therefore calls us to look at Jesus because He wants us to look at the human side of the Lord. Obeying God according to His nature is His divine side. But despising shame and enduring the cross for the sake of the joy set before Him is His human side. The Holy Spirit inspired the writer to call Him Jesus here, thus revealing to us the fact that the matter of reward had its influence on the Lord so far as the human side was concerned. True, we obey God because we love Him. But there is another side to this as we realize that God uses reward to encourage us to be faithful to Him. And hence it cannot be wrong for us His children to serve faithfully for the future reward.

Why does Paul say, "forgetting the things which are behind, and stretching forward to the things which are before, I press on toward the goal"? His own answer is that he might gain "the prize of the high calling of God in Christ Jesus" (Phil. 3.13,14). Since reward is what God calls men to obtain and since it is also that which Paul forsakes everything to gain, God must be pleased if we serve faithfully for the sake of reward.

Our Lord has "despised" and "endured" for the sake of the joy of the kingdom. How about us? Have we forsaken anything for the sake of the glory of the future kingdom? Have we done what we do not want to do or not done what we do want to do because of God's reward? If this joy could attract our Lord, why can it not attract us? Countless believers, both ancient and modern, have forsaken all to follow the Lord for the sake of the glory of the kingdom; how about you and me?

Seven

The Jesus whom we look to is the One who for the joy which was set before Him "endured the cross, despis[ed] shame, and . . . sat down at the right hand of the throne of God'' (Heb. 12.2b). In principle, we must run the same course as He did.

Shame is given to Jesus by men; yet this He despises. A cross is given Him by God; but this He endures. He is not perturbed by men's misunderstanding, ostracism, accusation, desertion, or condemnation. Not because the shame is not serious; in point of fact, the shame He suffers exceeds that which no other man has ever passed through. Neither is it because His holy nature is insensitive to the shamefulness of being insulted; actually His feeling is much keener than that of others. Nonetheless, Jesus despises the shame and disregards the insult. The cross which God has given Him is not light. What He has gone through before men and the evil spirits and the holy angels is not without hardship. Yet our Lord endures the cross. He accepts it and endures it. And the final result? He reaches the end triumphantly: ''and hath sat down at the right hand of the throne of God'' awaiting the moment of His glorious appearing.

In contrast to the Lord, though, how tenaciously we try to preserve our face. We are afraid of shame, misunderstanding, criticism and opposition from men. We endeavor to please all men. We avoid shame, not willing to deny our self nor suffering shame for the Lord's sake. And even when others are successful in putting us to shame, we bear it grudgingly. We are unwilling to accept without voice or protest the shame which decreases self-life.

Moreover, the cross which God gives we are unwilling to bear. We have not walked in the way of the cross. We do not even know what the way of the cross is. We do not realize that all which comes our way is permitted by God. Whatever is against our will, whatever causes us to be misunderstood, makes us suffer, blocks our way, or shatters our hope is a cross given by God to us. Yet how do we face such a thing? Do we resist in heart? Do we complain to people? Do we long to avoid these difficulties? Let us recognize that our lack of a submissive attitude will hinder us from running well.

Whenever God allows a cross to fall on us, He has a particular reason. Each cross has its spiritual mission, that is to say, it is sent to accomplish something special in our life. If we endure according to God's will—as the Lord Jesus endured the cross (noting, however, that *His* cross is to atone for sin whereas *ours* is not)—our natural life will be further dealt with and we shall have a greater capacity for being filled with the resurrection life of the Son. Our resistance, insubordination or struggle will hinder the success of God's purpose and thus cause the cross to fail in its mission.

Eight

God sets the Lord Jesus before us that we may follow Him. And in conclusion, God in His word tells us to "consider him that hath endured such gainsaying of sinners against himself, that ye wax not weary, fainting in your souls" (Heb. 12.3). We ought to consider carefully, point by point, how our Lord has endured reproach, oppression, ill-treatment, desertion, scourging, and crucifixion (the cross indeed has its human side). And in so doing we will not become weary. When the Lord spoke to His disciples about how He must suffer on earth, He said, "A disciple is not above his teacher, nor a servant above his lord" (Matt. 10.24). We cannot expect to receive better treatment than what the Lord Jesus experienced. And Jesus went on to say that "it is enough for the disciple that he be as his teacher, and the servant as his lord" (Matt. 10.25a). It is enough if the treatment we receive from the world is not more than what the Lord Jesus received, for "if they have called the master of the house Beelzebub, how much more them of his household!" (Matt. 10.25b) Since *He* received so much ill-treatment in the world, should not we also? And if we consider this matter, we will not wax weary in suffering shame and opposition.

In running the race of the kingdom, the one thing most dreadful is to become weary and faint in the soul. The soul is that part of man's being that embraces his emotion, mind and will. When the soul is weary and fainting, it loses its strength. Its will withers, its feeling chills, and its mind deadens. Everything becomes empty, we tend to let things drift, and the matter of a future crown is committed to fate. One great temptation in our running this race is to become loose and cease from running hard after the heavenly crown, as opposing forces seem to gather strength beyond the runner's endurance.

Yet if we truly consider the Lord Jesus and meditate on His experiences, we will not let ourselves loose. Recall the description given of Gideon and his

300 men: "faint, yet pursuing" (Judges 8.4). Though feeling faint, we must run.

May we be runners who run the race to the end. Even if during the running we may be wounded— having, from the hands of men, suffered opposition, misunderstanding and rejection—we must stir up our spirit and keep on running for the sake of the Lord Jesus. Who in a race will receive the most applause from men? Will it not be the one who has been wounded but who still keeps on running until he gains the first prize? Therefore, whether we be wounded or suffering or seemingly defeated, it ought not be a problem. It is still best for us to rise up and run. Let us remember that nothing counts while still on the road; only at the end of the course will judgment be rendered. Hence let us not forfeit the race for whatever reason. Let us not grow weary and become faint. On the contrary, we must look away to Jesus the author and perfecter of our faith, and run to the very end the race that is set before us.

3 | The Last Voyage

And straightway he constrained his disciples to enter into the boat, and to go before him unto the other side to Bethsaida, while he himself sendeth the multitude away. And after he had taken leave of them, he departed into the mountain to pray. And when even was come, the boat was in the midst of the sea, and he alone on the land. And seeing them distressed in rowing, for the wind was contrary unto them, about the fourth watch of the night he cometh unto them, walking on the sea; and he would have passed by them: but they, when they saw him walking on the sea, supposed that it was a ghost, and cried out; for they all saw him, and were troubled. But he straightway spake with them, and saith unto them, Be of good cheer: it is I; be not afraid. And he went up unto them into the boat; and the wind ceased: and they were sore amazed in themselves; for they understood not concerning the loaves, but their heart was hardened. (Mark 6.45–52)

This passage from the Gospel of Mark has often helped me in the past and continues to do so even today. Just prior to this incident the Lord Jesus is found feeding the five thousand with five loaves and two fishes. And after this same incident the Lord is seen healing many sick people. Together these three incidents form a composite type of the Lord Jesus with respect to the events from His death on the cross to His eventual establishment of the kingdom. They signify how the Lord (1) was crucified for us, (2) ascended to heaven to be the high priest for us, and (3) shall come again to set up the kingdom.

John also records the incident of our Lord's feeding the five thousand; except that in his Gospel more words were recorded as having been spoken. For after He had distributed the loaves and the fishes, our Lord is shown in John's account as having continued speaking to the same people the next day, presenting the following most important teaching: ''I am the living bread which came down out of heaven'' (John 6.51a). What He meant was that as they had just the day before eaten the loaves and were satisfied, so they must eat His flesh and drink His blood in order to have eternal life. And thus this incident of distributing the loaves typifies how the Lord was to die for them and us by having His body broken and His blood shed.

Mark 6.46 indicates that the Lord Jesus then ''departed into the mountain to pray''—this time typifying His ascension to be our high priest so that He might intercede for us before God.

And finally, the contents of Mark 6.53–56 constitute a type of the coming again of the Lord to establish His kingdom and heal all the sick.

But let us now focus on the matter of how the Lord commands the disciples to cross the sea, keeping in mind that this event stands between that incident which represents the cross and the one typifying the kingdom. And hence we can say that this central event applies to our own day—to the church age—and can therefore show us what will happen after the time of the cross but before the kingdom comes, and can also indicate what kind of attitude we must have. Here we will not lay stress on what the Lord has done for us but will instead emphasize what we ourselves ought to be doing.

"And straightway he constrained his disciples to enter into the boat, and to go before him unto the other side to Bethsaida, while he himself sendeth the multitude away" (v.45). First of all, this verse tells us that there is the Lord's way for every one of us. The word "constrained" here is the same word found in 2 Corinthians 5.14 ("for the love of Christ constraineth us"). The Lord constrains the disciples to enter the boat. In other words, the picture that can be visualized by these types is that once having died for them, the Lord constrains His followers to begin their voyage. The Lord sets a way for the disciples to go and commands them to traverse it. The most important thing in a Christian's life is to find out the ordained way of the Lord and to walk in it faithfully. Unfortunately, on the one hand, many believers have not discovered what is the respective way appointed to each of them, while on the other hand some who *have* dis-

covered the way fail to walk in it. No wonder their
lives are so passive and restricted and the work of
God suffers so much conflict and contradiction.
What is most needed for each one of us is to hand
ourselves over to God prayerfully, quietly and sub-
missively, to seek with singleness of heart direction
from Him as to His prescribed way, and to walk in
His will wholeheartedly, ready to pay any cost.

From Luke 9.10 we know that the place of the dis-
tribution of the loaves was Bethsaida. In looking at
the map, however, we note that there are two
Bethsaidas—the one being located to the northeast of
Capernaum and the other to the southwest of Capernaum. The Lord commands the disciples to depart
from northeastern Bethsaida and cross over to south-
western Bethsaida.

"And after he had taken leave of them, he departed into the mountain to pray" (v.46). This verse
is a picture of how our Lord was soon to leave His
earthly followers and ascend to the right side of the
Father to do the work of intercession. He leaves His
own on earth for them to run the course which He has
apportioned to them.

"And when even was come, the boat was in the
midst of the sea, and he alone on the land. And seeing
them distressed in rowing, for the wind was contrary
unto them, about the fourth watch of the night he
cometh unto them, walking on the sea; and he would
have passed by them" (vv. 47–48). What do the disciples encounter along the way the Lord appointed for
them? "And when even was come"—that is to say,
the sky darkens as the boat is on the sea. In type we

can say that Christ as the light of the world has already departed from this world. At His coming again, though, He shall be the Morning Star and the Sun. From the time of His ascension to the time of His coming again, the history of the world is but one long dark night. According to man's view the world is becoming better and brighter; but according to the word of God "the night is far spent" (Rom. 13.12). God has not said the world is getting better and brighter; on the contrary, He declares that the night is far spent. We are now in that dark night, and hence can sense darkness all around. Are you aware of the darkness around you? If you do not know what darkness is, nor are conscious of the darkness around you, you probably have been assimilated into the world. But if we walk in the light and live close to God by abiding in Christ, constantly judging the works of the flesh and obeying the leading of the Holy Spirit, we will most naturally perceive that this is truly a dark world.

"The boat was in the midst of the sea"—Our voyage has not arrived at its destination yet. Although the question of eternal life or eternal death is already settled beyond any doubt, our history on earth—as to whether we are faithful to the end or are variously changing in the way—is a matter which remains to be seen. Before the boat reaches the harbor it is subject to change and open to danger. We should never be so self-assured as to think that our destiny is already decided. Although it is a subject for rejoicing that we are on the voyage, the issue as to how we sail and its ultimate outcome remains a question.

What else do the disciples encounter on the way? They were "distressed in rowing, for the wind was contrary unto them," says the Scripture. Obviously, if the direction you are traveling is *against* the wind, then the opposite direction must be *with* the wind. And so, in the case at hand, the Lord's disciples, who travel from northeast to southwest, find the wind against them; whereas had they been travelling from southwest to northeast the wind would have been with them. Too many Christians only sail with the wind. It makes me wonder whether they are on the appointed way of the Lord. Let us accept the fact that we must go the way ordained for us, since the Lord has already decided for us our place in the world; for did He not say that "the world hated [His disciples]" (John 17.14)? So that the wind of this world is against our way. If we have never been opposed, ridiculed or persecuted by the world, we most likely are not standing in the place of the Lord's appointment. Now and then we should have encountered a contrary wind instead of our always having sailed with the wind. Because they go in the direction the wind blows, many believers do not realize that the world is at enmity with them nor can they understand why it was that the Lord suffered opposition on earth. But were they to sail according to the Lord's given direction from northeast to southwest, they would without doubt meet up with a contrary wind.

"Distressed in rowing, for the wind was contrary unto them"—Every faithful believer must have had the same experience. In recent years temptations seem to have increased both in number and in severity.

Those who are the Lord's appear to suffer much. The body is frequently weak and is often wracked with sickness. Families encounter endless problems and conflicts. Occupation and livelihood are becoming more difficult. Oppression—and even attack—from both society and nation are increasing in even greater measure. Satan and his evil spirits are stirring up many troubles to wear out the saints. Oh how great today are the contrary winds. Now if you stand in the Lord's appointed way, you will invariably sense the contrary wind. And how hard it must be!

Look, for example, at the situation in the church. What has been happening during these most recent years? All kinds of heresies have become rampant in the work of the church. The deception of the evil spirits has greatly increased. And the church has become more worldly than ever before. In such an age as this, are you able to sail against the wind and feel no distress if you proceed without turning aside from the ordained way of the Lord?

It is better to suffer than to drift. Far better is it to be distressed in rowing than to sail with the wind, far better is it to go the difficult way than to go the easy way and drift. Drifting consumes no energy. Stop rowing and the wind will send us back to where we first began. Just compromise a little, let go somewhat, and the wind will send us back. To love the world requires no effort; to follow the world demands no strength. But to stand and be faithful to the Lord is a sure invitation to an encounter with a contrary wind, and soon we shall feel distress in rowing.

It is quite easy to return to the old place, but quite

demanding of us to go forward. Yet now is the time to be faithful. May we walk in God's appointed way.

Please notice next that the disciples row the boat from evening to the fourth watch of the night. Whereas the Jews have three watches, the Romans (for whom Mark's Gospel is most likely aimed) have four. Now the beginning of the fourth watch is at three o'clock in the morning. The Lord's disciples keep on rowing, for they cannot go back, nor can they find relief in nearby Capernaum.

The period of the fourth watch is obviously the darkest hour during the entire night and it also brings an end to the night. Now it is just such a time as this that we must press on. I well realize that we all have temptations and trials. Nowadays temptations rage so fiercely that it is no time to condemn anybody. Yet the greatest peril today is to cool off a little, to compromise somewhat, or to take a brief nap—for we are really tired. At the beginning there was strength to stand, for we were under the constraint of love. But the intervening period has now become so long and the struggle has grown so very difficult that it is easy to become cold. How many believers I have known who years ago were so full of spirit and so brave in battle but who have now cooled down and drawn back because the wind is too much against them. One brother once commented that he rarely sees people any more who are still zealous in the Lord's work after fifty years of age. Cooling off one's ardor and faithfulness somewhat is a thing harder to overcome than all other temptations. To overcome sin is possible, but not to become cold after growing weary from constant sailing against the wind is almost impossible.

If at the beginning the Lord has constrained us and commanded us to go this way, if the Lord has ordered us to cross the sea to the other side, can we cease to advance? Yet should we indeed stop, the current and the wind will send us away even farther from the Lord. Let us suffer rather than drift.

At this point, though, what we need is some encouragement from the Lord, even as Paul encouraged Timothy: "I put thee in remembrance that thou stir up the gift of God, which is in thee . . . " (2 Tim. 1.6). May our first love be stirred up. The writer of the Letter to the Hebrews apparently sensed that some of the brethren "seem[ed] to have come short of it" (4.1)—that is to say, their first love towards the Lord seemed to have diminished. And so he went on later in the Letter to exhort them to "lift up the hands that hang down, and the palsied knees" (12.12).

Mr. Moule, who at one time labored in China, once said that the secret to great success in God was to be able to persevere to the very last half hour. Though the darkness is heavy, it will not last forever, for does not Isaiah 21.12 tell us that "the watchman said, The morning cometh, and also the night . . . "? It is now the dark night, but soon the morning shall come. Do please persevere to the last half hour. Let not our eyes dwell on the dark night nor on the difficulties, but let us steadily advance. It does not pay not to proceed forward today. It does not pay to grow loose now. For almost immediately the other shore shall be reached.

Mrs. Jessie Penn-Lewis has noted that many believers have declared in their personal testimonies that they have encountered many oppressions in their lives. Let me add in agreement that today's battle seems to be heavier day by day, as if the sole target of Satan's attack is we believers ourselves. So that in our age the current problem is whether you and I can persevere to that final half hour. "And [Satan] shall wear out the saints of the Most High" (Dan. 7.25). To "wear out" is to consume *slowly*. Far more difficult is it for us to recognize Satan as one who wears out the saints than Satan as one who is like a roaring lion. And yet his work of slowly consuming the saints has already begun.

Whenever I have been in Kuling Mountain, I have often walked along the stream that is there. Frequently I saw rocks as large in size, but as concave in their centers, as wash basins. This was due to the daily rubbing of the many small pebbles against them. In the same way Satan treats the children of God. Instead of killing them with one stroke, he tries to wear the saints down day by day so that without their knowing it they shall be severely wounded after some period of time.

Although we may have suffered much already, will we be able to persevere just a little while longer? Can we stand with the Lord up to the last half hour? Can we not watch with the Lord for one hour? (cf. Mark 14.37) Today is our time to stand firm. How pitiful it is if some have never encountered a contrary wind. If anyone has never known the world as bitter and corrupted and oppressive, he must not even have begun his voyage. Only when we walk faithfully will we feel the blowing of an adverse wind. But only then, too, will we be tempted by a voice that says, It is too much, relax a little and rest for a while. Let me observe, though, that it does not pay to rest now, because you and I have already covered quite a distance.

"And he [was] alone on the land. And seeing them distressed in rowing, for the wind was contrary unto them, about the fourth watch of the night he cometh unto them, walking on the sea; and he would have passed by them"—The Lord is watching to see if we persevere or if we change. He waits to see whether we go forward or go backward. His eyes are upon you and me. He notices every step of our way. And He well knows how great are our temptations and how difficult are our circumstances. Yet He will not let us suffer beyond the fourth watch. At the time of the darkest hour the Lord will come: for has He not already died for us, and has He not ascended to heaven to pray for us, knowing all our trials? But when the sky is *darkest*, He *shall* return.

In verse 48 something very special is mentioned. It states that the Lord "would have passed by them"! Many people are surprised when they read this: it seems as if the Lord is not going to the disciples. But actually there is no problem here. For since the Lord orders His disciples to go to the other side—to the other Bethsaida—then to Bethsaida will He naturally go upon coming down from the mountain. The Lord will not go somewhere else to wait for them. He seeks them in the very way which He has commanded the disciples to travel. Now if they had turned aside, the

Lord would not have met them nor turned aside to wait for them. How serious this is. I sometimes wonder if the Lord were to order me to be in Shanghai but I were to go instead to Nanking, whether I would be raptured when the Lord comes? For rapture takes place in the way of the Lord's appointment. And will I not miss the rapture if I am not there? Each one of us is responsible for where he is.

"And he went up unto them into the boat, and the wind ceased"—As soon as the Lord comes, everything is all right. Praise and thank God, that though the wind is contrary it will not forever be so; that though the rowing is hard, there will not be rowing forever. Perhaps the Lord is already on the way. We must agree that we *can* endure sufferings on earth because behind us the Lord has died for us and before us the Lord is coming again. We have the love of Christ constraining us at the back and we have the hope of His return drawing us from the front. A missionary once declared: I have the Lord as my portion, therefore I *can* forsake all things. The eyes of the Lord are upon us, therefore let us not be afraid to suffer. In the event we now turn aside for fear of suffering, all our past sufferings will be in vain.

One who was deeply spiritual in the Lord once wrote:

When we read 2 Thessalonians 2.3 and 2 Timothy 3.1–13, we know before the day of the coming of the Lord there will be apostasy and perilous days when the wicked and deceptive shall greatly increase. Such apostasy does not refer to education, mass meetings, capable pastors, gorgeous cathedrals, and mental and physical advances. It is related to faith and the recognition of the power of God. It points to well-known churches which incline to so-called Higher Criticism (actually it equals to unbelief), and deny the supernatural works of God such as regeneration, holiness, answers to prayers and the revelation of the Holy Spirit.

Before the day of the coming of the Lord, there will arise great deception and error; and if it be possible, even the elect shall be deceived. The 'form of godliness' shall be increased. Faith shall be decreased due to false beliefs engendered by Satan, and also the love of the world and the denial of God's word. One brother said it well: Such Satanic works shall produce an intangible effect which will surround us as the air. It will create a form of outward godliness, but its inside is filled with the wicked spirits and the melancholies of hades. These wicked spirits will do their best to hurt, to mislead and to oppress God's children. They will attack our body, suppress our will and deaden our thoughts. All sorts of strange sensations and trials will come upon us, causing us surprisingly to lose the desire for and the strength towards God, having found our spirit tired, thought dulled and will drowsy, and at the same time oddly to love the pleasures and customs of the world as well as covet the forbidden things of God. We lose the freedom and power of preaching; we cannot concentrate on listening to messages; and we are unable to kneel and pray earnestly for long. Such darkness and such atmosphere we must resolutely resist. No doubt Satan seeks to darken our mind and will with a kind of inconceivable power so as to make it extremely difficult for us to walk with God but to render it very easy to live according to the flesh. We find it hard to serve God faithfully and pray persistently, as if everything within us rises up to hinder us from following the Lord Jesus to the end and to entice us to agree with the world.

The atmosphere around us presses us to defect from God and to desist from earnest prayers. It tends to dull our spiritual senses so that we may not see heavenly realities or the glorious presence of the Lord. Thus will we easily neglect the communion with God and find ourselves hardly able to keep up fellowship with God.

We have already felt the beginning of these influences upon us. Worldly lusts weave their spreadout net in many forms around believers. It becomes tighter and stronger as time goes on. Many things which in the former generation were unthinkable are now being done and without shame. Many places of worship not only resist spiritual things and block revivals but also introduce all kinds of feastings and doubtful things into them.

Generally speaking, everywhere in the world shows the decrease of faith and the increase of apostasy. Of course, we acknowledge that there are yet many places which are blessed by God. But looking at the situation of the church in the entire world as a whole, it cannot fail to present a woeful picture.

Having seen these things, we cannot help but cry to the church of God to rise up, to stir up, to return to commune with God, and to please the Lord with the time which yet remains. Let us be prepared to stand before the judgment-seat of Christ and present our case.

What this servant of the Lord expressed above is true. I do not know how you feel. But as for myself, I feel daily that the whole world is against us. We can only have two attitudes: one is to persevere, the other is to relax. The world welcomes you to return, and Satan is pleased if you go back. But the Lord commands you to cross over to the other Bethsaida that is on the other side. If we are not faithful now, we will never be faithful at all. Many of God's children truly suffer for the Lord's sake, and they travel on the lonely path. Shall we be as a brother in England once wrote: Others pass over to the Lord through bloody seas, but would we go to the Lord in a flowery sedan chair? Moses said to the children of Gad and the children of Reuben, "Shall your brethren go to the war, and shall ye sit here?" (Num. 32.6) Can we sit immovable while others faithfully suffer? Suffering, yes; but it is better than drifting. Every one of us must serve the Lord faithfully and proceed on the way which He has commanded us until we reach the other shore.

TITLES YOU
WILL WANT TO HAVE

by Watchman Nee

Basic Lesson Series
Volume 1—A Living Sacrifice
Volume 2—The Good Confession
Volume 3—Assembling Together
Volume 4—Not I, But Christ
Volume 5—Do All to the Glory of God
Volume 6—Love One Another

The Testimony of God
The Salvation of the Soul
The King and the Kingdom of Heaven
The Body of Christ: A Reality
Let Us Pray
God's Plan and the Overcomers
The Glory of His Life
"Come, Lord Jesus"
Practical Issues of This Life
Gospel Dialogue
God's Work
Ye Search the Scriptures
The Prayer Ministry of the Church
Christ the Sum of All Spiritual Things
Spiritual Knowledge
The Latent Power of the Soul
Spiritual Authority
The Ministry of God's Word
Spiritual Reality or Obsession
The Spiritual Man
The Release of the Spirit

ORDER FROM:

Christian Fellowship Publishers, Inc.
11515 Allecingie Parkway
Richmond, Virginia 23235